Teacher's resource

150

Literacy Hour

YEAR 6

Lessons

Contents	Page

Acknowledgements

The author and publisher would like to thank the following for permission to reproduce material in this book:

The play of 'The Goalkeeper's Revenge' by D. Nicholls and R. Speakman, reproduced with the permission of Heinemann Educational. 'The Voyage of The Matthew' © John Crace first published in The Guardian, June 1997. Extract from 'The Eighteenth Emergency' by Betsy Bryars published by Bodley Head. Used by Permission of the Random House Group Limited. 'Tom's Midnight Garden' by Philippa Pearce (first published 1958) reproduced with the permission of Oxford University Press. 'Pigeons' by Richard Kell (from 'Differences') reproduced with the permission of Chatto and Windus 'Once there were Dragons' by John Mole reproduced with the permission of Scholastic Books. 'Through that Door' by John Cotton (from 'Two by Two') reproduced by permission of the author and the publisher, HarperCollins Ltd. 'The Pink Bow Tie' by Paul Jennings (from 'Thirteen Unpredictable Tales') reproduced with the permission of Penguin Books. 'Eggs' by Miriam Moss reproduced with the permission of A&C Black (Publishers) Limited. 'Wind' by Ted Hughes (from 'Hawk in the Rain') and 'Macavity: The Mystery Cat', 'Skimbleshanks: The Railway Cat', 'Bustopher Jones: The Cat about Town' by T.S. Eliot (from 'Old Possum's Book of Practical Cats') reproduced with the permission of Faber & Faber. 'The Octopus', 'The Pig', 'Reflection on Ingenuity' and 'The Cow' by Ogden Nash (from 'Candy is Dandy') reproduced with the permission of André Deutsch Limited.

The following titles are in the public domain but the publisher acknowledges the use of extracts from the following material:

'The Mistletoe Bough' by Thomas Haynes Bayly, 'Silver' by Walter de la Mare, 'Requiem' by Robert Louis Stevenson, 'The Railway Children' by E. Nesbit, published by Penguin Books. 'A Christmas Carol' by Charles Dickens, 'Jabberwocky' by Lewis Carroll, 'Voyage to the Centre of the Earth' by Jules Verne.

Every effort has been made to trace and acknowledge ownership of copyright material but if any have been inadvertently overlooked, the publisher will be pleased to make the necessary alterations at the first opportunity.

First published 2001
exclusively for WHSmith by

Hodder & Stoughton Educational,
a division of Hodder Headline Ltd.
338 Euston Road
London NW1 3BH

Text and illustrations © Hodder & Stoughton Educational 2001

A CIP record for this book is available from the British
Library.

Author: Chris Lutrario
Series editor: Gill Matthews

ISBN 0340 79001 6

Typeset by Fakenham Photosetting
Printed and bound in Spain by Graphycems

Each term is divided into ten weekly themes, organised as follows:

• Objectives for the week
These are taken from the National Literacy Strategy Framework for Teaching and form the basis of medium term planning for text, word and sentence level work.

• Resources
A list of the materials that are needed to teach the theme. Some themes are generic and a range of texts could be used while others are written around suggested texts.

Where necessary, preparation that can be carried out in advance is highlighted.

• Assessment
This is an outline of broad assessment objectives, recognising that many teachers already have detailed recording and assessment procedures in place in their schools.

• Lesson outlines
Each lesson is divided into the following sections:

Whole class
This section contains suggestions for whole class shared reading or writing activities. The final outcome of most themes is a completed piece of written work. The whole class teaching aims to guide children through the objectives in order to achieve this.

Group and independent work
This section contains ideas for group work, whether guided by you or another adult, or independent work. The suggested activity may be the task that you focus on with a group. How these activities are used will depend on your particular organisation.

Differentiation
Most lessons are accompanied by differentiated activities for high and low attainers and suggestions for where it would be suitable for children to work in mixed ability pairs.

Whole class
The final section of each lesson gives ideas for a plenary session, including:
- activities which revisit key learning objectives;
- feedback from children, either individuals, pairs or in some cases the whole class, on the work they have been doing;
- feedback from children on a partner's work;
- preparation for the next day's lesson
- class evaluation of a lesson or a theme of work.

• Photocopiable masters (copymasters)
Most themes are accompanied by photocopiable masters for use in whole class and group time. These are not work sheets to practise taught skills, but are closely linked to the content of the lesson. Many can be used as frames for collecting discussed ideas or for shared writing in whole class sessions, as well as by the children in group or independent work.

• Homework
Each theme is accompanied by a photocopiable homework sheet which explains to parents or guardians what the children have been doing in literacy work for that particular week. This is followed by a task that can be carried out by the child.

Throughout the themes the development of reading and writing skills are linked closely. Themes or blocks of themes start with an emphasis on the teaching of reading through shared reading, use the reading as a stimulus or model for shared writing and suggest ideas for children's writing based on the shared work that has been carried out.

Shared reading

The different reading organisations covered include:
- teacher reading to the children;
- children reading with the teacher;
- class reading without the teacher joining in;
- a group reading to the rest of the class;
- individual children reading to the class.

Shared writing

This book suggests activities whereby teachers model writing, provide a scaffold to support children in their writing and teach writing over a sequence of lessons. Children's writing should be used in shared sessions as a means of encouraging the early stages of drafting and improving writing.

Word level work

In order to ensure the appropriate emphasis and

focus it is often better to introduce word level work separately from text level work. Teachers will lead children in using their word level skills within shared reading and writing.

• Phonics

Phonic work should be used to support reading and children should be encouraged to see links between phonic activities and shared and guided reading activities. Phonic work should also be incorporated into shared writing activities. Children can be encouraged to use word lists generated in phonic work to help with spellings. Many children find a class-made 'long vowel' dictionary a useful writing support.

• Word recognition, graphic knowledge and spelling

Word walls, lists and cards are ways of displaying and drawing children's attention to words that need to become part of their sight vocabulary. Recognition and practice of these words can be incorporated into shared and guided work.

• Handwriting

Most schools have adopted a particular handwriting scheme and many teachers have taken the practising of handwriting out of the Literacy Hour. However, modelled and shared writing provide good opportunities to demonstrate handwriting.

Teaching and learning strategies

A range of teaching techniques are suggested to make lessons interactive and ensure the involvement of all children. These include:

- Use of the 'time out' strategy during whole class sessions where pairs or small groups of children are given short periods of time to discuss a question, think of an appropriate word or compose a sentence.
- Pairing children during group work to encourage discussion and develop collaborative skills.
- Feedback from the class when sitting in a circle.
- Use of small whiteboards. These can be purchased from suppliers or made by laminating card and used with appropriate pens.
- Many teachers now make use of large whiteboards for shared writing and related activities. Large sheets of sugar paper may be more appropriate for some activities as they can be:
  - displayed as a model for writing;

  - used as part of a 'work in progress' display;
  - referred to as a memory jogger;
  - re-read as a familiar text, which can be particularly useful for low attaining children.

Speaking and listening

A range of suggestions for the inclusion of speaking and listening are included, such as:

- organising a range of audiences for reading and for the sharing of written work;
- encouraging children to listen to each other in discussion about aspects of texts;
- asking children to respond to a range of questions, to give opinions and share ideas;
- making use of drama techniques such as 'hotseating', where some children are encouraged to take on a role and others to ask questions, during whole class work.

ICT

The amount of use made of ICT depends on many factors such as the hardware available and teachers' confidence in using it. A range of suggestions for its use are offered.

Word processing
The majority of writing activities that are carried out with paper and pencil can be fulfilled using a word processing package. Children's lack of word processing skills often makes tasks such as producing a final copy of a piece of written work laborious and time consuming. However, opportunities for word processing can be organised through tasks such as creating captions, labels, book titles and headings.

The Internet
The Internet may be used to find information relating to fiction and non-fiction work.

E-mail
There are a growing number of local, national and international projects making use of the school e-mail address to develop links with other groups and share information and ideas.

Word and sentence level activities
There are a growing number of programs available to support spelling development and the learning of certain grammatical structures.

Autumn term

	Theme	Objectives: children will be taught to:
1	Word roots and origins	Use known spellings as a basis for spelling other words with similar patterns or related meanings. Use independent spelling strategies; use known prefixes or suffixes; use awareness of meaning or derivation. Use word roots, prefixes and suffixes as a support for spelling. Understand the function of the etymological dictionary.
2	Classical poetry	Articulate personal responses to literature. Be familiar with the work of established authors. Write their own poems, experimenting with active verbs and personification; produce revised poems for reading aloud. Revise earlier work on verbs; understand the terms active and passive. Understand how words and expression have changed over time.
3	Structure and punctuation of complex sentences	Understand the terms active and passive; transform sentences. Note how changes from active to passive affect word order and sense. Investigate connecting words and phrases. Form complex sentences, using and evaluating different connecting devices. Secure knowledge and understanding of more sophisticated punctuation marks. Investigate the meaning and spelling of connectives.
4	Journalistic style	Comment critically on the language, style and success of examples of non-fiction (journalistic writing). Develop a journalistic style. Use the styles and conventions of journalism to report on real or imagined events. Use IT to plan, revise and edit writing. Revise word classes; re-express sentences in a different order. Form complex sentences. Secure knowledge and understanding of sophisticated punctuation marks.
5	Non-chronological reports	Comment critically on the language, style and success of examples of non-fiction (reports). Secure understanding of the features of non-chronological reports. Write non-chronological reports linked to other subjects. Revise work on verbs and understand the terms active and passive. Note and discuss how changes from active to passive affect word order. Investigate connecting words and phrases. Investigate meanings and spellings of connectives.
6	Playscripts	Compare and evaluate a play in print and the film/TV version. Contribute constructively to a shared discussion about literature. Prepare a short section of story as a playscript. Revise from Year 5: different word classes (adverbs, adjectives); the conventions of Standard English; adapting texts for particular purposes.
7	Classic fiction on screen and in print	Compare and evaluate a novel in print and the film/TV version. Articulate personal responses to literature. Be familiar with the work of some established authors. Contribute constructively to a shared discussion about literature. Prepare a short section of story as a script. Understand how words and expressions have changed over time. Revise construction of complex sentences; adapting texts for particular purposes.
8	Shakespeare	Compare and evaluate a play in print and the film/TV version. Be familiar with the work of established authors and know what is special about their work. Contribute constructively to discussion about literature. Read and examine biographical texts. Develop the skills of biographical writing. Investigate connecting words and phrases. Understand how words and expressions have changed over time.
9	Viewpoint in fiction	Take account of viewpoint in a novel; identify narrator; explain effect; consider other viewpoints. Articulate personal responses to literature. Be familiar with the work of established authors. Manipulate narrative perspective; write in the voice of a text; write a story with two narrators. Plan their own narrative writing. Revise word classes (pronouns). Adapt texts for particular purposes. Build spellings by syllabic parts; apply knowledge of spelling rules and exceptions; build words from other known words.
10	Biography and autobiography	Distinguish between biography and autobiography. Comment critically on the language, style and success of examples of non-fiction writing. Develop skills of biographical and autobiographical writing in role. Revise adapting texts for particular readers and purposes; revise word classes. Investigate connecting words and phrases. Research the origins of proper nouns (family names).

Summary of objectives

Spring term

	Theme	Objectives: children will be taught to:
1	Word roots and origins	Use known spellings as a basis for spelling other words with similar patterns or related meanings. Use independent spelling strategies; use known prefixes or suffixes; use awareness of meaning or derivation. Use word roots, prefixes and suffixes as a support for spelling. Understand the function of the etymological dictionary.
2	Commentaries and summaries	Analyse the success of texts. Write commentaries or summaries. Revise work on complex sentences. Revise work on contracting sentences (summary, note making). Use known spellings as a basis for spelling other words. Use independent spelling strategies.
3	Genres in fiction	Identify key features of different types of literary texts. Analyse the success of texts and writers in achieving effects. Use different genres as models for their own writing. Study one genre in depth and produce an extended piece of similar writing. Parody a literary text. Use independent spelling strategies. Learn and invent spelling rules and mnemonics.
4	Humorous verse	Recognise how poets manipulate words. Investigate humorous verse. Increase their familiarity with the work of significant poets of the past. Use different genres as models for their own writing. Use known spellings as a basis for spelling other words.
5	Narrative structure	Understand aspects of narrative structure. Analyse how paragraphs are structured in writing. Analyse the success of texts. Write their own story using sophisticated narrative devices Revise work on contracting sentences (summary, note making).
6	Official language	Read and understand examples of official language and its characteristic features. Discuss the way that Standard English varies in different contexts. Investigate further the use of active and passive verbs. Understand features of formal official language. Revise work on complex sentences.
7	Poetic devices and effects	Recognise how poets manipulate words (for quality of sound, connotations, layers of meaning). Analyse how messages, moods, feelings and attitudes are conveyed in poetry. Read and interpret poems in which meanings are implied or multi-layered. Write commentaries. Revise work on complex sentences. Use known spellings as a basis for spelling words with similar patterns.
8	Poetic forms	Recognise how poets manipulate words. Identify key features of literary texts. Increase their familiarity with significant poets of the past. Use different genres as models for writing. Revise work on complex sentences. Understand that meanings of words change over time.
9	Proverbs	Identify the key features of different kinds of literary texts. Use different genres as models for writing. Revise work on complex sentences. Revise work on contracting sentences. Collect and explain the meanings and origins of proverbs. Understand that the meanings of words change over time.
10	Argument and discussion	Recognise how arguments are constructed to be effective. Identify the features of balanced written arguments. Construct effective arguments. Write a balanced report of a controversial issue. Investigate conditionals. Construct sentences which express possibilities and hypotheses.

Summer term

	Theme	Objectives: children will be taught to:
1	Word play	Use known words as a basis for spelling other words with similar patterns. Use independent spelling strategies. Invent words using known roots, prefixes and suffixes. Practise and extend vocabulary through word games. Experiment with language, creating new words.
2	Advertisements: a language investigation	Review a range of non-fiction text types and their characteristics. Select the appropriate style and form to suit a specific purpose and audience. Revise the language conventions and grammatical features of different tpe of text (persuasive). Conduct detailed language investigations. Practise and extend vocabulary. Experiment with language.
3	Comparing novelists and novels	Describe and evaluate the style of an individual writer. Compare and contrast the work of a single writer. Look at connections and contrasts in the work of different writers. Use a reading journal effectively. Compare texts in writing. Revise the language conventions and grammar of different types of text (narrative). Secure control of complex sentences.
4	Explanatory texts	Secure understanding of the features of explanatory texts. Identify the key features of impersonal formal language. Secure control of impersonal writing. Divide whole texts into paragraphs. Revise the language conventions and grammatical features of different types of texts (explanatory). Revise formal styles of writing. Identify mis-spellings.
5	Extended story writing	Write an extended story on a theme identified in reading. Annotate passages in response to specific questions. Revise language conventions and grammatical features of different types of text (narrative). Secure control of complex sentences. Identify mis-spelt words. Use independent spelling strategies. Practise and extend vocabulary. Experiment with language (similes and metaphors).
6	Linked poems	Discuss how linked poems relate to one another. Comment critically on the overall impact of a poem. Annotate passages in detail. Compare texts in writing. Write a sequence of linked poems. Revise formal styles of writing. Secure control of complex sentences. Experiment with language (similes and metaphors).
7	A range of non-fiction texts	Identify the key features of impersonal language. Review a range of non-fiction text types and their characteristics. Secure control of impersonal writing. Divide whole texts into paragraphs. Select the appropriate style and form to suit a specific purpose and audience. Revise language conventions and grammatical features of different types of text. Revise formal styles of writing.
8	Reference texts	Appraise a text quickly and effectively and retrieve information from it. Secure the skills of skimming, scanning and efficient reading. Select the appropriate style and form to suit a specific purpose. Revise formal styles of writing. Use independent spelling strategies: dictionaries and IT spell-checks. Practise and extend vocabulary.
9	Reviews	Describe and evaluate the style of an individual writer. Write summaries of books or parts of books. Write a brief synopsis of a text. Write a brief, helpful review, tailored for real audiences. Select the appropriate style and form to suit a specific purpose and audiences. Revise formal styles of writing. Practise and extend vocabulary.
10	A study of an individual poet	Describe and evaluate the style of an individual poet. Comment critically on the overall impact of a poem. Compare and contrast the work of a single writer. Annotate passages in detail. Write a brief and helpful review for real audiences. Revise formal styles of writing. Practise and extend vocabulary.

Theme 1) Word roots and origins

Objectives

Word level:

- 2 to use known spellings as a basis for spelling other words with similar patterns or related meanings
- 3 to use independent spelling strategies: use known prefixes and suffixes; use awareness of meaning or derivation
- 5 to use word roots, prefixes and suffixes as a support for spelling
- 10 to understand the function of the etymological dictionary

Resources

Sophisticated dictionaries, including ones which include information about word derivations; an etymological dictionary, and dictionaries including brief information about word origins.
Copymasters 1 and 2, Homework 1

Assessment

At the end of this theme is the pupil able to:
- analyse polysyllabic words, identifying word roots and more complex prefixes and suffixes;
- understand the meaning of some Latin and Greek word roots;
- spell these word roots accurately;
- draw on this knowledge to spell new words;
- use dictionaries to find the derivation of words?

Lesson 1

Whole class

Explain that in this unit they will be finding out about the derivations and origins of words, and learning how to use this knowledge to support spelling. This first lesson concerns prefixes: remind children of the meaning of this term.
Write up words beginning with the prefix super, *e.g. supernatural, supersonic, superior, supervise, superficial, supermarket*. Ask children what they notice about their structure and meaning; draw out the idea that they all begin with the same prefix and contain the sense of 'over' or 'beyond'.
Divide the class into pairs or small groups; give each group another prefix *e.g. auto, trans, sub, inter, multi, pre, ex, com*; ask them to list words beginning with this prefix, and then to work out its meaning and how it is applied in each case. After about five minutes, give groups a dictionary to help their search. Ask a group to present their words; explain how knowing the prefix and its meaning helps with spelling.

Group and independent work

Children continue to search for and record words beginning with prefixes introduced in whole-class work, and others. Present these as posters, *e.g. using web diagrams or lists*.

Differentiation

Low Attainers – Find and write down three words beginning with each of six prefixes.
High Attainers – Scan dictionary for prefixes not already introduced; identify their meanings; list words.

Whole class

Ask children to share collections of words beginning with the same prefix, identifying its meaning.
Organise a short prefix spelling test; swap work, and mark answers.

Lesson 2

Whole class

Explain that in this lesson they will be looking at words including roots from Latin. Link this with work in History on the Roman occupation of Britain.
Write up words including the Latin root 'port', *e.g. transport, portable, export, import, report, porter*. Ask children to define the meaning of each word, and then deduce the meaning of the common root (to carry). Note how the addition of prefixes and suffixes extends this meaning.
Write up other words which include commonly used Latin roots, *e.g. equal, primary, local, compartment, pedal, construct, revise*. Brainstorm and record words that include these roots; work out their meaning.
Explain and demonstrate how this can help with spelling: words with the same roots/meanings have the same spelling pattern, no matter how they are pronounced, *e.g. visor and vision, partial and particle*. Identify words in which this is the case.

Group and independent work

Assign a Latin root to individuals or groups; ask children to find as many words as they can that include it, and to write a dictionary definition for each.

Differentiation

Low Attainers – Record pairs of words with the same Latin root; identify the shared meaning.
High Attainers – Copymaster 1. Sort words with less common roots into pairs; work out meaning of root; add another word.

Whole class

Ask children to read their definitions: can the others work out the word?
Ask children who have worked with less common or obvious roots to present their list of words: can the others work out the shared meaning? Note cases in which the root is pronounced differently but spelt the same.

Lesson 3

Whole class

Explain that in this lesson the children will be looking at English words including word roots from Greek. Link this with work on the Ancient Greeks in History or on their gods and myths in English.

Write up words including the root phon, e.g. phoneme, phonics, telephone, symphony, xylophone, stereophonic, microphone. As in Lesson 2, ask children to define each word and identify the meaning of the root. Note how this is extended by other parts of the word, e.g. xyl = wood, stereo = solid.

Write up other words which include commonly used Greek roots, e.g. geo (earth), graph (writing), photo (light), chron (time), hydr (water), opt (eye), psych (mind). Brainstorm and record words that include these roots; work out their meaning.

Note pronunciation of unusual spelling patterns, e.g. ph as f, ps as s, ch as hard c, which indicate words of Greek origin. List words including them.

Group and independent work

Revisit the activity from Lesson 2, assigning words with Greek roots.

Differentiation

Low Attainers – Ask children to find and record another word including each of the roots introduced in whole-class work.
High Attainers – Encourage children find other Greek roots, and to use the language conventions of definitions.

Whole class

Ask children who have found 'new' roots to share their sets of words: can others work out the common meaning?
Organise a spelling of words including Latin and/or Greek roots. Swap work, and mark.

Lesson 4

Whole class

Write up the pairs of words unicorn and monorail; duet and bicycle. Ask children what the words in each pair have in common; explain that the first refers to things with one of something and the second with two. Identify the word roots: uni and du from Latin; mono and bi from Greek. Record other words that include these roots.

Work through words related to numbers three to ten, a hundred and a thousand: prompt children to contribute words (giving clues where necessary), and identify the Latin and Greek roots, which are sometimes the same and sometimes different: 3 tri; 4 quad or quart/tetra; 5 quint/penta; 6 sext/hex; 7 sept/ hept; 8 oct; 9 non or nov; 10 dec; 100 cent/hect; 1000 mill/kilo.

Use words from this and the previous lessons to demonstrate how to analyse the structure of words as an aid to spelling. Draw vertical lines to show prefix/root/suffix. Identify and explain related spelling rules, e.g. dropping final e of root, as in monotonous.

Group and independent work

Divide class into 12 groups; assign each a number (1 to 10, 100, 1000) to work with. Ask them to find, list and define words which include the Greek/Latin roots for their number. Present their work as a poster, illustrating objects.

Differentiation

Low Attainers – Work with numbers referring to 1 or 2; present as a picture dictionary.
High Attainers – Write full dictionary definitions.

Whole class

Count round the class, asking groups to contribute a word referring to 1, 2 ,3, etc. Pause on interesting words; prompt children to define them, note their structure, and any unusual or tricky spellings.

Lesson 5

Whole class

Choose a word the children have not met in this theme but which includes Greek or Latin roots, e.g. manuscript, aqueduct, quadruped, bilingual, astronaut, disaster, vivisection, thermometer, microscope. Explain that there is a kind of dictionary that explains the origins of words; introduce the terms etymology, etymological.

Demonstrate the process of 'looking up' and researching the chosen word. If possible, present the entry as an enlarged text; explain what information is included and how it is presented.

Give pairs or small groups a copy of this dictionary or a non-specialist dictionary which includes basic information about word origins. Write up a list of other new and interesting words with Greek or Latin roots (see above); give children five minutes 'time out' to research them.

Ask them to share their findings; mark up and annotate words to show their meaning and origin.

Group and independent work

Set children task challenges using dictionaries with etymological information. e.g. new words including a root studied in the unit; words from languages other than Latin or Greek; words from specific languages.

Differentiation

Low Attainers – Copymaster 2. Children research words with clear, interesting origins.
High Attainers – Scan the first few pages of a particular letter; note origins of words; make general observations.

Whole class

Ask questions which prompt children to share particular findings, e.g. Who has found a word from X? from Y? A new Latin or Greek root? Who has any ideas about where words in the English come from? About the kind of words originating in a particular language?

Theme 2) Classic poetry

Objectives

Text level:
- 3 to articulate personal responses to literature
- 4 to be familiar with the work of established authors
- 10 to write own poems, experimenting with active verbs and personification; produce revised poems for reading aloud

Sentence level:
- 2 to revise earlier work on verbs; understand terms active and passive

Word level:
- 7 to understand how words and expressions have changed over time

Resources

Collections of classic poetry in single author and mixed anthologies; enlarged text versions of contrasting classic poems which include words no longer commonly in use and which make use of personification (e.g. Christina Rossetti's 'Is the Moon Tired?'; Sara Coleridge's 'The Months'). Copymasters 3 and 4, Homework 2.

Assessment

At the end of this theme is the pupil able to:
- understand and respond to a range of classic poems, identifying significant aspects of content, effect and style;
- draft and revise poems which use personification;
- understand the role of active, powerful verbs in poetry;
- identify and comment on examples of language change over time?

Lesson 1

Whole class

Explain that in this theme the children will be studying poems by famous poets of the past. Read (but do not show text of) the first poem to the children. If it is short, read it again. Give them a couple of minutes to respond to the poem individually and silently by jotting down ideas, questions, words or phrases that struck them, or by making quick sketches of images. Share these first impressions, first with a partner, then with the whole class. Note ideas on the board.

Display the enlarged text version of this poem; re-read it while the children follow the text. Prompt them to refine and extend their ideas and answer their questions by reference to the detail of the text. Focus their attention on key aspects of language and structure: rhyme pattern, rhythm, imagery, word choice, organisation in lines and verse. Identify any words, phrases and structures that are no longer in use. Make notes under these headings.

Group and independent work

Children read and closely examine another classic poem, and make notes under the headings suggested above. Towards the end of this phase, ask children to prepare a brief oral introduction for their poem.

Differentiation

Low Attainers – Work with a short, accessible poem; focus on a small number of striking features.

High Attainers – Copymaster 3, make notes about a poem under headings; develop this as a short non-chronological report.

Whole class

Ask children to introduce their poem to the rest of the class, describing and explaining what they noticed about its content and style; and then to read it aloud.

Lesson 2

Whole class

Display enlarged text version of the second classic poem, choosing one which makes use of personification and contrasts in language and structure with the first. Read the poem to the children while they follow the text.

Give pairs of children their own copy of the poem. Ask them to re-read it, and to highlight parts they find interesting, unusual or puzzling.

After about five minutes, draw the class together again, and work through the poem line by line, encouraging children to share what they noticed. Use the enlarged text to model and explain focuses and techniques for annotation.

Focus in on the use of personification in the poem. What inanimate phenomenon is being seen as human (or animal)? What effect does this create? Identify the words which make this comparison, looking in particular at the use of active verbs (e.g. winds that sigh; grass that whispers). Record these.

Group and independent work

Children read other classic poems that use personification, write a brief commentary on the two sides of the comparison and list the words used to create the effect, noting the part of speech of each.

Differentiation

Low Attainers – Show the comparison visually, and list the relevant words.

High Attainers – Scan anthologies for poems that use personification, and write short comments on them.

Whole class

Ask children to describe the personifications they found. Choose one or two examples to develop: ask children to read the relevant lines and list the words used to create the comparison. Again, draw attention to the role of verbs.

Lesson 3

Whole class

Show again the enlarged texts from Lessons 1 and 2, and ask: How could you tell that the poems were written in the past? Prompt children to identify and comment on aspects of content and sensibility that suggest the age of the poem; then focus in on any words and phrases that are no longer in use. Make a list of these. Work out their meaning, and identify modern equivalents.

Supplement this by sharing other poems or verses which include 'old' words and expressions. Discuss as above and add to the list.

Read through the list and ask children if they can detect any categories of language change over time, e.g. *different verb and pronoun forms, words that refer to things no longer in use, words that are still sometimes used but with a consciously archaic effect (yonder)*. If possible, reorganise the list in sets.

Group and independent work

Children read other classic poems, identify 'old' words and expressions and write glossary entries explaining their meaning, modern equivalents, and (where appropriate) the nature of the language change involved.

Differentiation

Low Attainers – Copymaster 4. Identify 'old' words in a poem

High Attainers – Draw together work on a number of poems to comment more generally on language change over time.

Whole class

Organise children to share and explain examples of language change of the kinds identified in whole-class work. Add words to the lists or sets.

Lesson 4

Whole class

Briefly review the work on personification from Lesson 2. Draw up a list of the phenomena or objects personified, and add to it. Subjects with potential include months and seasons; weather conditions; the sea; moon, stars and sun. Give children five minutes 'time out' to work in pairs to choose a phenomenon or object and to brainstorm how it could be seen as human: what kind of person? doing what? You could extend the idea of personification to include seeing things as animals.

Ask children to share ideas; choose one to develop with the class.

Use shared writing techniques to draft a short poetic description. An effective way of doing this is to begin by stating the likeness (The X is a Y), and then develop the personification in more detail. This produces a simple poetic structure which the children can use as a model for their own writing. Focus on the use of verbs: If the X was a Y, what would it do? List suitable verbs.

Group and independent work

Children use personification to write their own descriptions of an inanimate object or phenomenon, following or elaborating the model introduced in whole-class work.

Differentiation

Low Attainers – Use a simplified version of the model: statement of likeness plus two sentences expanding this.

High Attainers – Challenge children to use other aspects of the language of the poems they have been studying.

Whole class

Ask children who have written about the same phenomenon to introduce and share their writing. Compare the work: What have they likened it to? How have they developed the comparison?

Lesson 5

Whole class

Choose, from the previous lesson and with their authors' permission, one or two pieces to revise and develop. Present these as enlarged texts. Read them to the class, or ask the authors to do this. Ask everyone (author included) to think of some features of the writing that work well and others that could be improved or developed. Highlight and annotate the text to show this. Work together to revise the piece. Choice of words, especially verbs, is likely to be a crucial issue here: What words could be used to make the likeness more vivid and striking? To achieve a particular effect? List alternatives, try them out in the piece, and choose one to use. As the rewriting proceeds, look for opportunities to shape the writing as a poem, e.g. *organising it in lines, adjusting words to give a pattern of rhythm.*
Write out a new version of the piece.

Group and independent work

Children revise the descriptions they wrote in Lesson 4, paying special attention to word choice. Encourage children to extend their work, e.g. *by writing a sequence of personifications of different months or different weather conditions.*

Differentiation

Low Attainers – Mark up and annotate first draft for or with them, suggesting possibilities for improvement and extension.

High Attainers – Challenge children to develop their pieces more fully as poems.

Whole class

Invite children to introduce and read their work, explaining what they changed and added and why. Look for opportunities to develop the language issues raised, e.g. *word choice, structuring in lines.*

Theme 3) Structure and punctuation of complex sentences

Objectives

Sentence level:
- 2 to understand terms active and passive; transform sentences
- 3 to note how changes from active to passive affect word order and sense
- 4 to investigate connecting words and phrases
- 5 to form complex sentences, using and evaluating different connecting devices
- 6 to secure knowledge and understanding of more sophisticated punctuation marks

Word level:
- 6 to investigate meaning and spelling of connectives.

Resources

A selection of texts, some in enlarged versions, which include sentences with complex structures, sophisticated punctuation and a variety of connecting words and devices. Word cards for the sentences composed in Lesson 1.
Copymasters 5 and 6, Homework 3.

Assessment

At the end of this theme is the pupil able to:
- identify whether sentences are in the active or passive voice;
- transform sentences form active to passive and vice versa, understanding changes in word order and meaning;
- link and combine ideas clearly in longer, more complex sentences using a range of connecting words and devices;
- use sophisticated punctuation to mark boundaries in complex sentences and make their meaning clear?

Lesson 1

Whole class

Explain that in this unit the children will be investigating the structure and punctuation of sentences. The focus of this first lesson is active and passive sentences.
Ask a child to perform a simple action; use the cards to compose an active sentence describing it, *e.g. Jack put the pencils in the pot.* Explain that there is another way of describing the action; rearrange and change the words to show the passive form: *The pencils have been put in the pot (by Jack).* Introduce or revise the terms active and passive; identify differences in verb form, word order and emphasis. Ask children to compose similar pairs of sentences.
Similarly, transform a passive sentence into the active; note changes and added information.
Identify and read brief extracts from kinds of writing *e.g. impersonal reports of experiments, non-chronological reports* in which the passive voice is typically used, and discuss why (personal opinions are of less importance).

Group and independent work
Children write pairs of active and passive sentences about the same event. Search for examples of these two kinds of sentences in books they are reading.

Differentiation
Low Attainers – Use a set of word cards to make a limited number of matching active and passive sentences.
High Attainers – Use passive voice to write a short report of a recent investigation or experiment.

Whole class
Ask children to share active/passive sentences they have found in their reading. Ask others to identify which it is; confirm, identifying features of each.
Share pairs of sentences, identifying changes in word order and verb form.

Lesson 2

Whole class

In this lesson the focus is on linking ideas in and between sentences. Write up a few very short sentences each stating one fact about a familiar topic. Ask children to think about how these sentences could be joined to make a more coherent account. Give them a few minutes 'time out' to explore this in pairs, then share ideas. Write up and develop possibilities, drawing attention to the use of conjunctions; words that link clauses (who, which, where …); turning sentences into phrases (e.g. 'He travelled on horseback' becomes 'Travelling on horseback …'). Discuss and evaluate these different ways of linking ideas.
Show enlarged text versions of extracts from a chronological text (*e.g. instructions, recount*) and a non-chronological text (*e.g. report, argument or discussion*). Prompt children to identify the connecting words and devices used in these two genres, and to note differences: i.e. use of temporal connectives in the former and of connectives indicating logical relationships in the latter. Compile two lists of connectives; add more of a similar kind to each list.

Group and independent work
Children compose brief texts of one of the kinds investigated above, on a subject of their own choice. Continue to display the list of connectives for reference.

Differentiation
Low Attainers – Copymaster 5. Cloze activity in which children supply missing connectives.
High Attainers – Write in one of the more challenging non-chronological genres.

Whole class
Ask children to read out an example of each genre; ask others to put up their hands when they hear a connective. Write up and examine sentences which use connectives in effective or interesting ways.

Lesson 3

Whole class

Explain that the focus in this lesson is on combining information in sentences, using punctuation for parenthesis.

Write up a sentence stating one simple fact, *e.g. Tom lost his hat*. Ask children to suggest ways in which this could be elaborated by adding information about Tom. Then give them a couple of minutes to compose new sentences, orally or in writing. Share and write up some of these sentences. Contribute some of your own. Underline phrases and clauses that add parenthetical information, *e.g. Tom, my best friend, lost ...; Tom, who lives next door to me, lost ...* Explain how commas, dashes and brackets are used to demarcate these phrases or clauses. Develop, alter and repunctuate sentences as needed.

Repeat the process, this time adding to the original sentence information about Tom's hat and how he lost it. Combine information to develop a longer and more complex sentence; experiment with reordering clauses or phrases, and identify changes in effect, especially the emphasis given to information that comes first.

Group and independent work

Write up other simple, one-fact sentences; ask children to write new sentences which include more information. Five minutes before the end of this phase, ask them to check that their sentences are accurately punctuated.

Differentiation

Low Attainers – Add just one new item of information to each sentence.

High Attainers – Copymaster 6. Add clauses at beginning, middle and end of two simple sentences.

Whole class

Monitor independent work to select sentences which illustrate key teaching points on sentence structure and punctuation. Write up and investigate the structure and punctuation of these sentences. Explore alternatives, and note difference in effect.

Lesson 4

Whole class

Show and read through an enlarged text in which a colon is used in at least one sentence. Ask children to identify and comment briefly on all the punctuation marks used, then focus in on the colon. Introduce the term. Prompt children to work out its function in this case. This could be one of three: to introduce a list (but not generally when this follows a verb); to introduce a quotation; to explain or expand on information stated in the first part of the sentence.

Explain the other uses of the colon. Write up the beginning of sentences which illustrate each of these functions (*e.g. X was beginning to worry: ... There are three things I like about winter: ... The first sentence grabs your attention:*). Work with the children to write continuations for each sentence.

Group and independent work

Children search in books for sentences punctuated with colons; identify which of the three functions it is used for. They can then write a sentence for each of these functions.

Differentiation

Low Attainers – Write their own continuations for the sentence openings used in whole-class work.

High Attainers – Write sentences about a favourite book and author, using colons in different ways.

Whole class

Ask children to contribute examples of sentences with colons they have found; ask others to identify the function.

Ask children to share own sentences in which they have used a colon to introduce a list; confirm correct usage. Repeat for other two uses.

Lesson 5

Whole class

Show and read through an enlarged text in which a semi-colon is used in a sentence with two clauses. Introduce the term. Prompt children to discuss the function and effect of this way of punctuating the sentence. Draw out the idea that semicolons are used to link clauses that are closely related in meaning. Repunctuate the sentence, making each clause into a separate sentence. Note how the link becomes weaker. Introduce and explain another use of the semi-colon: to separate longer items in a list. Work with children to write a list in which each item is a single word, *e.g. favourite colours, punctuating it with commas*. Write another list in which items consist of phrases and/or clauses, some punctuated with commas, *e.g. favourite activities: I like swimming in the sea, especially when it is raining; going to the cinema with Amy, who ...* Punctuate with semicolons, noting that commas could be confusing.

Group and independent work

Children search in books for sentences punctuated with semi-colons; experiment with alternative ways of writing the sentence. Then write a simple list; elaborate it by adding more information about some of the items; and use semi-colons to punctuate it.

Differentiation

Low Attainers – Punctuate sentences by inserting missing colons and semi-colons in the right places.

High Attainers – Write their own sentences which need to be punctuated with semi-colons.

Whole class

Work together to add punctuation marks, including colons and semi-colons, to a text where they are missing. Consolidate and extend knowledge of the functions of these punctuation marks, and how they mark the grammatical structure of sentences.

Theme 4) Journalistic style

Objectives

Text level:
- 12 to comment critically on the language, style and success of examples of non-fiction (journalistic writing)
- 15 to develop a journalistic style
- 16 to use the styles and conventions of journalism to report on real or imagined events
- 18 to use IT to plan, revise and edit writing

Sentence level:
- 1 to revise word classes; re-expressing sentences in a different order
- 5 to form complex sentences
- to secure knowledge and understanding of sophisticated punctuation marks

Resources
A collection of stories and reports from local and national newspapers; an enlarged text version of a newspaper report which exemplifies the language and structural features noted below.
Copymaster 7 and 8, Homework 4

Assessment
At the end of this theme is the pupil able to:
- identify and comment on the characteristic features of journalistic writing;
- use these features in their own writing;
- write complex sentences which are clear, grammatically correct and accurately punctuated;
- consider alternative ways of ordering and linking ideas in complex sentences?

Lesson 1

Whole class

Explain that in this theme the class will be exploring the language of newspaper reports.

Display the enlarged text newspaper story, and read it through with the children. Prompt them to discuss its content (Is it clear? interesting?) and the viewpoint of the writer (Is it purely objective? Or does the journalist express his/her own opinion?). Identify and highlight relevant sections of the text.

Ask children to re-read the report, and then give them five minutes to share ideas in pairs about its style and structure.

Pool ideas as a class. As the discussion develops, prompt the children to focus on headlines, opening sentences and the structure of the 'story'. (Each of these will be studied in detail in the following lessons.)

Group and independent work
Pairs of children read other newspaper stories, and make notes about the aspects of content and style discussed in the whole-class phase. If possible give them copies which they can mark up and annotate.

Differentiation
Low Attainers – Children work with shorter and simpler reports and/or use a prompt sheet.
High Attainers – Children work with longer and more complex reports.

Whole class
Ask pairs to comment on the content, interest and appeal of the newspaper stories that they have examined, and whether the journalist expresses an opinion on the events. If so is this explicit or implicit? Prompt them to read out sections of the text which illustrate their points.

Lesson 2

Whole class

For the following three lessons, pairs of children need the newspaper stories they read in Lesson 1.
Share some headlines, and write them up on the board. Prompt children to discuss the function of headlines, and how effective they are in these cases. Do they give a good idea of the story? Do they make you want to read on?
Switch the focus to the language of headlines, asking children what they notice about how words are used. Draw their attention to the use of short words; the omission of words (especially articles and verbs); the use of nouns as adjectives (e.g. CIRCUS DEATH SHOCK). This provides a good context for revising word classes. Be ready to contribute headlines which exemplify these features. Rewrite some of the headlines in a longer, more conventional form, noting changes. Ask children to imagine that the events of Cinderella actually took place. What would be a good headline for the

newspaper story? Experiment with alternatives, focusing on word use.

Group and independent work
Children write headlines for real or fictional stories, *e.g. personal or school events; episodes from novels they are reading*. Encourage them to experiment with different possibilities. Pairs could use a computer with maximums set for line length and font size.

Differentiation
Low Attainers – Copymaster 7. Write headlines for well-known traditional tales and nursery rhymes.
High Attainers – Write alternative headlines for the same story; work within given limits, *e.g. only four words; only 20 characters*.

Whole class
Share a headline for a traditional tale; challenge children to compose a shorter or more eye-catching headline for the story.
Share another headline. Ask children to identify the class of each word used and words that have been omitted.

Lesson 3

Whole class

Ask children to share some opening sentences from the newspaper stories they have been reading. Choose one which exemplifies the characteristic features (see below), and write it on the board.

Ask children what they notice about the style and structure of this sentence, and what its function is. Typically, such sentences introduce the key facts of the story and are densely packed with information. They therefore tend to be long and complex, and often include several clauses and/or phrases requiring internal punctuation. Identify and discuss structure and punctuation of these sentences. Experiment with different ways of ordering the information.

Ask children to write (on a wipeable board or jotter) the opening sentence for a newspaper report on the story of Cinderella. Share examples; experiment with reworking. Look for opportunities to draw attention to how punctuation marks can be used to mark the structure of the sentence.

Group and independent work

Children write opening sentences for the real or fictional stories they wrote headlines for in Lesson 2. Encourage them to experiment with different ways of organising the information they want to include.

Differentiation

Low Attainers – Start by writing a list of the facts they want to include; you could provide this for them.
High Attainers – Copymaster 8. Rewrite opening sentences, responding to editor's comments.

Whole class

Share some opening sentences. Choose one to write up. Experiment with its content and structure, *e.g. adding or deleting an item of information; moving an item from one position to another; fine tuning the punctuation.*

Lesson 4

Whole class

Display the enlarged text newspaper story again. Re-read it; make notes on the function and/or content of each paragraph, *e.g. 1: introduction; 2: elaboration of main event; 3: information about main person involved.*

Ask them what they notice about how the story is organised. Provide a clue by asking: How does it differ from the organisation of a fictional story? Draw out the idea that newspaper stories are typically organised according to the importance of the information (starting with the most important and moving towards background information) rather than chronologically. Ask children how the story of Cinderella might be organised if it were a newspaper story (*e.g. her marriage to the prince would come first; information about the remarriage of her father later*). Record 'topics' for the first few paragraphs.

Ask children why this might be (readers want to know the most important things first).

Group and independent work

Pairs of children re-read their newspaper story and record its structure. They then make a plan for the real or fictional story they have been working with, organising it as a newspaper report.

Differentiation

Low Attainers – Write key events of a traditional tale on pieces of paper; reorganise as a newspaper report.
High Attainers – Reconstruct their newspaper report as a chronological narrative.

Whole class

Ask children who have been reorganising familiar fictional stories to present their plans, and to begin retelling the story to this structure. Ask others to comment on the different effect. Can they see other, more effective ways of organising the material?

Lesson 5

Whole class

Explain that in this lesson the children will be pulling together work from previous lessons to write their own newspaper story about a real event that has taken place recently in the school, locally or nationally.

Brainstorm possibilities for this. Choose one for the class to work on together. Give children a couple of minutes to invent headlines; experiment with changing words, reordering, shortening. Choose one to use. Similarly, compose opening sentences for this story. Write up and experiment with alternative starting points and structures; check the punctuation. Choose one. Next, work together to plan the structure of the story, paragraph by paragraph. As the work proceeds, look for opportunities to extend understanding of the features of journalistic writing and to revisit the issues of objectivity and viewpoint.

Group and independent work

Children work, individually or in pairs, on their chosen story. Where possible, organise children to use computers, and to experiment with columns and different font styles and sizes. This activity provides a context for extended writing in further literacy hours or outside this context.

Differentiation

Low Attainers – Complete the newspaper story begun in the whole-class phase.
High Attainers – Draft and revise their stories, developing a more complete and authentic journalistic style.

Whole class

Share 'work in progress' by displaying it or reading it out loud. Choose an example to focus on, and prompt children to discuss issues of clarity, interest and viewpoint and the extent to which it follows the conventions of journalistic style.

Theme 5) Non-chronological reports

Objectives

Text level:
- 12 to comment critically on the language style and success of examples of non-fiction (reports)
- 13 to secure understanding of the features of non-chronological reports
- 17 to write non-chronological reports linked to other subjects

Sentence level:
- 2 to revise work on verbs and understand the terms active and passive
- 3 to note and discuss how changes from active to passive affect word order
- to investigate connecting words and phrases

Word level:
- 6 to investigate meanings and spellings of connectives

Resources
A collection of non-fiction books including examples of non-chronological reports. Enlarged text version of a non-chronological report exemplifying the characteristic text- and sentence-level features of the text type, in particular connectives and passive sentences. Copymasters 9 and 10, Homework 5

Assessment
At the end of this theme is the pupil able to:
- identify and comment on the text- and sentence-level features of non-chronological reports;
- identify use of active and passive constructions;
- transform sentences from active to passive and from passive to active;
- use connectives to link ideas in their writing clearly;
- spell connectives accurately;
- write non-chronological reports, using structural and language conventions effectively?

Lesson 1

Whole class

Explain that in this unit they will be finding out about a kind of non-fiction text: non-chronological reports. Share and discuss a book or section of a book of this text type. Ask children to identify the main subject, and, by looking at contents and headings, how information about this subject is organised. Draw out the idea that the author focuses and organises the material in 'parts' which correspond to significant aspects of the subject. Contrast this with chronological reports or recounts in which organisation is largely dictated by the order of events in time.

Display and read an enlarged text version of a section from this book; prompt children to identify and describe language features, in particular use of present tense (indicating 'this is how things are'); impersonal language (author's perspective not highlighted); language that generalises (all rather than particular cases); use of connectives. Annotate the text to show these features.

Group and independent work
Children look at other examples of non-chronological reports; make notes about how the material is organised; identify characteristic language features in a particular section. Towards the end of this phase, ask children to be ready to share what they have found out.

Differentiation
Low Attainers – Photocopy, cut up and muddle headings and paragraphs from a non-chronological report; children order them.
High Attainers – Work with more complex texts; identify a sentence which illustrates the language features.

Whole class
Ask children to describe how material is organised in the non-chronological report they have been examining. Share and write up examples of typical language use.

Lesson 2

Whole class

Display enlarged text from a non-chronological report including passive sentences. Identify and underline these sentences. Ask children what they notice; provide a clue by rephrasing in the active voice. Draw out the idea that in passive sentences the agent or 'doer' of the action is not stated (*A cure for the common cold has been discovered in a laboratory in Scotland*) or occupies a less prominent position in the sentence (*... discovered by scientists in a ...*). Discuss why sentences of this kind are often used in non-chronological reports: the personal agent is of less importance than what happens.

Write up active sentences, and ask children to rework them in the passive; they could use white boards. Highlight changes in word order and verb form, especially use of were/was and been. Reverse the process, reworking sentences from passive to active; this sometimes involves deducing or guessing the agent.

Group and independent work
Children identify and record sentences in the passive voice in the non-chronological reports they read in Lesson 1. Then write pairs of sentences in passive and active voices. (A good context is mishaps and excuses: *The paint has been spilt; X spilt the paint.*)

Differentiation
Low Attainers – Copymaster 9. Rework simple active and passive sentences.
High Attainers – Try reworking the passive sentences they find in non-chronological reports.

Whole class
Ask children to contribute passive sentences they have found. Check and confirm this, noting relevant aspects of sentence structure and meaning.
Share matching pairs of active and passive sentences; write them up; identify differences in verb form and word order.

Lesson 3

Whole class

Display enlarged text from a non-chronological report including several connecting words and phrases. Read the text with the children; pause at and underline the first connective. Ask the children to identify and comment on the function of this word or phrase. Draw out the idea that it links ideas in the sentence; identify the nature of the link in this case (e.g. *indicating a contrast, a similarity, a consequence, a supporting point, an example*). Link with earlier work on conjunctions.

Ask the children to read on independently, and to jot down the connectives. Share these, and identify the kind of link they make. Compile a list.

Ask children in pairs to compose and write other sentences including some of these connectives. Pool suggestions for other connecting words and phrases; identify their function; add to the list.

Group and independent work

Children read other non-chronological reports; identify and record connecting words and phrases. They then write sentences including them.

Differentiation

Low Attainers – Write sentences including five simpler connecting words; or complete sentences which stop at a connective.

High Attainers – Copymaster 10. Categorise connectives from whole-class work.

Whole class

Ask children to share and explain sentences with connectives they have found and written themselves. Prompt discussion of why these particular connectives are often found in non-chronological reports. Organise a connectives spelling test; check answers together.

Lesson 4

Whole class

Introduce a subject with which children are familiar, e.g. *animals, bridges, towns and cities.* Brainstorm and record significant aspects of the subject. (*E.g. for animals: habitat, body parts and features, food and feeding, reproduction, etc.; for bridges: location, building materials, type of construction, transport using.*)

Explain that this is the kind of focusing and organising of material that underpins a non-chronological report. Develop this into a series of headings which would form a plan or framework for a non-chronological report about the chosen subject. Choose one of these headings, and discuss whether there would be sub-headings within this and, if so, what.

Prompt children to consider what might be missing from a report with just these headings. Draw out the idea that non-chronological reports also generally include an introduction, providing a brief overview of the subject and setting the scene for what follows.

Group and independent work

Children choose a subject for a non-chronological report of their own; brainstorm and record 'areas' within it; develop from this a structure of headings and sub-headings to serve as a plan for writing. Present this on a large sheet of paper.

Differentiation

Low Attainers – Define and write headings for four main areas within their subject.

High Attainers – Define and write sub-headings to further organise some of the main sections they have identified.

Whole class

Ask children to show and talk through their plans, explaining how and why they have organised the material in this way. Prompt the whole class to discuss the clarity and completeness of the plan.

Lesson 5

Whole class

Choose an area within the subject discussed in the previous lesson. Write up the heading and any sub-headings. Give children a few minutes to compose the first few sentences for this text, in their heads or in writing. Draw on these ideas to begin drafting the first section of the report. Read it through. Prompt children to consider whether the text exhibits the language features of non-chronological reports identified in Lessons 2 and 3. Focus in particular on the consistent use of impersonal language, the present tense and generalisation. Note points at which connectives could be used to make links between ideas clear. Revise the draft. Repeat this composition process for the following sections of the report.

Group and independent work

Children begin drafting the non-chronological report they planned in Lesson 4. This works well as a group activity with children drafting different sections, then revising and editing together. It offers an opportunity for extended writing, across a series of literacy hours in which you revisit the teaching points, within and/or outside this context.

Differentiation

Low Attainers – Write just two or three sentences, in the appropriate style, under each heading and sub-heading.

High Attainers – At the revision stage, give children a list of features of non-chronological reports against which they can check their work.

Whole class

Remind children of one of the features of non-chronological reports; ask them to share a sentence which illustrates their use of this feature. Confirm that this is the case. Repeat with other features. Revise or extend teaching of these features, as appropriate.

Theme 6) Playscripts

Objectives

Text level:
- 1 to compare and evaluate a play in print and film/TV version
- 5 to contribute constructively to shared discussion about literature
- 9 to prepare a short section of story as a playscript

Sentence level:
- 1 to revise from Year 5: different word classes (adverbs, adjectives); the conventions of Standard English; adapting texts for particular purposes

Resources
Playscripts in which dialogue includes examples of colloquial and non-standard English;
a video recording of a film or TV version of one of these plays, or dramatised performance on audiotape;
enlarged text versions of extracts from playscripts; a selection of familiar novels and short stories.
Copymasters 11 and 12, Homework 6

Assessment
At the end of this theme is the pupil able to:
- read and respond to playscripts, and understand the characteristic features of the genre;
- identify and comment on the conventions of standard English and on non-standard forms;
- adapt a section of narrative text as a playscript, using the conventions of the genre;
- explain the function and use of adverbs?

Lesson 1

Whole class

Before the lesson, organise a group to prepare a 'read through' of an episode from the chosen playscript. Ask this group to present their performance while the rest of the class follow the text, presenting some of it in enlarged form.
Ask the class to say which parts of the script were not read aloud and why. Use their response to this question as the starting point for identifying and discussing the conventions of the genre: the divisions of the text into Acts and Scenes; the description of setting at the start of each scene; stage directions; indications of expression, often in the form of adverbs (angrily, falteringly); list of characters, often with brief descriptions.
Highlight and annotate the enlarged text to show and name these features.

Group and independent work
Children read on into the next scene of this playscript or begin reading another. Discuss and make notes on use of conventions and on the development of plot, theme and character. Prepare a 'read through' performance.

Differentiation
Low Attainers – Follow the text of this playscript while they listen to a taped reading.
High Attainers – Read a different playscript, and compare with one read in whole-class work.

Whole class
Ask a group that worked with the original playscript to present their performance of the next scene while the rest of the class follow the text. Share (sensitive) comments about how they interpreted the text, focusing in particular on response to stage directions and indications for expression.
Continue discussion of playscript conventions.

Lesson 2

Whole class

Re-read a section of playscript from Lesson 1. Prompt children to identify examples of colloquial or non-standard English and any phonetic representations of speech (*e.g. 'at for hat*); highlight these if you are using an enlarged text. Discuss the more formal and standard equivalents, and why authors sometimes write in this style and use these forms. You could develop this by looking at a passage from a novel which includes dialogue in non-standard English.
Focus on the use of adverbs to indicate how actors should speak their lines. Use this as the starting point for revising the function of adverbs, how adjectives can be transformed into adverbs by adding the suffix ly, and spelling patterns related to this, *e.g. angry/angrily; gentle/gently.*

Group and independent work
Children return to the playscripts they read independently in Lesson 1, and identify and list examples of colloquial and non-standard English and adverbs to guide performance. Then list as many adverbs as they can to describe how people speak.

Differentiation
Low Attainers – Read playscript on Copymaster 11; circle and list adverbs; add other adverbs to the list
High Attainers – Read playscript on Copymaster 12; identify non-standard forms and write standard equivalents.

Whole class
Ask children to share any other examples of non-standard English they have found; discuss standard form. Play an adverb game: one child speaks or performs a mimed action in a particular manner (*e.g. writing quickly*); the others guess the adverb that describes it. Write the adverb on the board, explaining relevant spelling rules.

Lesson 3

Whole class

Organise the class to watch a recording of a film or TV performance of the chosen play (or to listen to an audiotape). Focus in particular on the episode they have been reading in the previous two lessons. Show this part again, and ask the children to follow the text.

Display an enlarged text version of some or all of this episode and use highlighting and annotation to identify and comment on features of the performance.

Prompt children to discuss how the text has been dramatised. How closely have the author's stage directions, descriptions of setting etc. been followed? Focus their attention on aspects such as setting, action, mood, the characters' appearance and the depiction of their personalities. Is this what they expected from reading the text? What other, better ways of interpreting and dramatising the text can they see?

As the discussion develops, encourage them to refer to the playscript to develop and support their ideas.

Group and independent work

Children watch or listen to another scene from the play; on a second viewing, they could make notes. They then take on the role of theatre critics, and write a short review of the performance.

Differentiation

Low Attainers – Identify and comment on two things they like about the performance and two things they think could be improved. Give the performance a star-rating.
High Attainers – Encourage children to refer in their review to the detail of the text.

Whole class

Ask some children to read their reviews, and the others to comment on them, sharing personal responses, expressing, explaining and justifying their opinions.

Lesson 4

Whole class

Choose, from a familiar story, an episode which includes several characters, some action, and a good deal of dialogue. Read it with the children, presenting at least the start of it as an enlarged text.

Explain that they are going to turn this into a playscript. Ask them to draw on their knowledge of the story to list adjectives that describe each character; use these as the basis for writing character descriptions. Similarly, list adjectives to describe the setting for the scene, and write a description. Discuss how the scene will start: what will happen first? Who will speak first? What will they say? Prompt children to refer to the text of the story.

Together, write the beginning of the scene, following the conventions of the genre and including stage directions etc.

Group and independent work

Individuals or groups write the first draft of a playscript version of an episode from a story of their own choice – this could include one which they have written themselves.

Differentiation

Low Attainers – Provide a writing frame with names of characters and space alongside for dialogue.
High Attainers – Suggest an episode which provides a particular kind of challenge for adaptation as a playscript.

Whole class

Ask children to share ideas about the process of adapting stories as playscripts. What problems did they face? How did they overcome them?

Ask individuals or groups to read their playscripts. Prompt them to identify and discuss ways in which the original story has been adapted, and how successful this is.

Lesson 5

Whole class

Choose (with the individual's or group's agreement) a draft playscript to share with the class. If possible, present it as an enlarged text. Read this aloud; then ask the other children to 'perform' it, taking parts individually or in groups. (Include a narrator to read sections which are not dialogue.) Ask the class to identify and comment on aspects of the playscript which they think work well and aspects which they think are less successful, explaining reasons for their views. As the discussion develops, prompt them to focus on the features of the genre (Lesson 1); on the use of adverbs to guide performance; and on the inclusion of colloquial and non-standard forms (Lesson 2). Discuss ways in which the playscript could be improved; and rewrite or amend sections.

Group and independent work

Children share playscripts in their groups, discussing strengths and weaknesses and possibilities for improvement. They then write a second/final draft.

Differentiation

Low Attainers – 'Mark' the first draft before the lesson, making suggestions for revision.
High Attainers – Read and re-read the dialogue aloud as they work; focus on fine tuning it.

Whole class

Ask groups to read and perform the scenes they have written; then explain some of the things they changed between first and second drafts, and why. Ask the 'audience' to comment (sensitively) on how well the scene works. Discuss possibilities for staging the scene more fully, *e.g. using costumes, scenery, lighting.*

Theme 7) Classic fiction on screen and in print

Objectives

Text level:
- 1 to compare and evaluate a novel in print and the film/TV version
- 3 to articulate personal responses to literature
- 4 to be familiar with the work of some established authors
- 5 to contribute constructively to shared discussion about literature
- 9 to prepare a short section of story as a script

Word level:
- 7 to understand how words and expressions have changed over time

Sentence level:
- 1 to revise construction of complex sentences; adapting texts for particular purposes

Resources

A video recording of a TV or film adaptation of an appropriate classic novel, e.g. *A Christmas Carol, Black Beauty, Treasure Island, The Wizard of Oz, Alice in Wonderland*; the text of this novel or a substantial extract from it; other classic novels.
Copymasters 13 and 14, Homework 7

Assessment

At the end of this theme is the pupil able to:
- identify and discuss differences between film/TV and print versions of the same story;
- express personal response to literature in discussion with others;
- identify and understand some features of the work of an established author;
- adapt part of a story for film/TV presentation, including writing of a playscript;
- identify and comment on examples of language change over time?

Lesson 1

Whole class

Select an episode from the chosen novel to study in screen and print versions. (Set work on this unit in context by reading the novel or a substantial part of it to the children.)
Explain that they will be looking at how written stories are turned into films and television programmes.
Read the chosen episode to the children, presenting some or all of it as an enlarged text. Ask them to share ideas and responses with a partner. Then discuss as a class.
Identify distinctive features of plot, theme and language, and spot clues that the story was written in the past. Identify and list words or phrases that are not in current use; discuss modern equivalents. Look for differences in sentence structure and punctuation.

Group and independent work

Children read on in this or another classic novel/extract. They make notes as they read and/or discuss in their group, focusing on issues raised in whole-class work. Use Copymaster 13 to record 'old-fashioned' words and their modern equivalents.

Differentiation

Low Attainers – Follow the text as they listen to the story read on tape.
High Attainers – Give children questions to encourage examination of the text at a deeper level, including language differences.

Whole class

Ask children to share ideas about the extracts they have read. Encourage them to develop the discussion of characteristic features and reasons why the book has achieved classic status. Discuss 'old-fashioned' words, and 'how we would say it' today.

Lesson 2

Whole class

Organise the class to watch the part of the film/TV version of the novel which includes the episode they read in Lesson 1. Suggest significant things to look for, and watch the tape again. Remind the children about the extract they read (with you and independently). Ask them: What do you notice about how it has been turned into film/TV? What has been changed? Added? Taken out? How? Why? Draw their attention to the (likely) absence in the film/TV version of the narrator's commentary and the description of action, setting and character. Prompt them to focus on aspects of film/TV 'language', e.g. *music and sound effects, camera angles, close-ups and long shots, lighting, editing.*
You could record ideas about the differences between the two versions in columns.

Group and independent work

Children re-read the text from Lesson 1, and make notes comparing and contrasting this with the film/TV version, developing and adding to points from whole-class work. (If possible, continue to replay the tape.) They could record ideas in two columns of balanced points.

Differentiation

Low Attainers – Complete pairs of sentences beginning *In the film/TV version ... In the book.*
High Attainers – Make notes under headings for aspects of fiction, e.g. *action, setting, characterisation, dialogue.*

Whole class

Discuss which version of the story they think is most and effective, and why. Encourage children to justify their views by comparing the two versions in detail. Look for opportunities to draw out general points about how the two media work and how readers/viewers interact and respond.

Lesson 3

Whole class

Chose an episode from the novel/extract which includes some dialogue. Read it with the children, presenting some or all of it as an enlarged text.

Briefly discuss the content and language of this episode (see Lesson 1), and the effect it creates on the reader. Ask children how they would adapt the episode in a film/TV version. What would they need to change? As the discussion develops, prompt them to focus on various elements of narrative form (*e.g. action, character, setting, dialogue*) and film 'language' (*e.g. music, sound effects, lighting, editing, camera angles*).

Annotate and mark up the enlarged text to show what might be deleted and changed, and where cinematic effects and techniques could be used.

Group and independent work

Children read this or an episode from another classic novel, and make notes about how they would adapt it for film/TV. If possible provide copies of text which they can mark up and annotate. Continue identifying words which are no longer in use; record them on Copymaster 13.

Differentiation

Low Attainers – Make notes under headings related to aspects of film language (see above).
High Attainers – Read and make notes on a different episode.

Whole class

Pool 'old-fashioned' words they have found in their extracts; identify and discuss their meaning, and modern equivalents.

Ask children to take on the role of film producers; they have to convince the rest of the class that the episode they have read would make a good film.

Lesson 4

Whole class

Draw some storyboard frames (see Copymaster 14) on the board, and explain how directors use these to work out a the sequence of 'shots' in a film, using sketches of what will appear on the screen and notes about lighting, sound, etc.

Recap the episode read together in Lesson 1, and use the storyboard to plan a screen adaptation. (If the episode is long or includes many events, choose one 'moment' from it to focus on.) Start with the first shot. What will it show? Make a rough sketch of this in the frame. How? What will be on the sound track? If there are actors, what will they do and say? Make notes under the frame.

Encourage children to refer to the text as they discuss the TV/film treatment.

Group and independent work

Children use Copymaster 14 to make a storyboard presentation of the episode they explored in Lesson 3. Organise this as a group activity in which children discuss the sequence together, and then make sketches and notes for a few shots individually.

Differentiation

Low Attainers – Work in visual images only.
High Attainers – Make more extended notes about film treatment.

Whole class

Display the storyboards around the room. Give the children a few minutes to look at them. Ask one group to present and talk through their storyboard, explaining how they adapted the text. Ask others who worked on the same episode to compare this with their treatment. How did they divide it up into shots? How did they 'treat' it?

Lesson 5

Whole class

Return to the episode and text used in Lesson 4, and focus with the children on the dialogue between characters. Highlight or underline this on the enlarged text. Discuss how the author uses dialogue here – *e.g. to develop character, to comment on the action.*

Identify and discuss ways in which the dialogue could be adapted for a film/TV version. Consider in particular whether any dialogue or surrounding text can be omitted because the actors could convey the information through expression and gesture.

Recap the conventions for writing playscripts. Use shared writing strategies to rework the opening exchanges in the episode as a play/filmscript, including stage directions where appropriate.

Group and independent work

Children write a play/filmscript version of the episode they presented in the previous lesson as a storyboard.

Differentiation

Low Attainers – Present dialogue in speech bubbles; these could be added to the storyboard.
High Attainers – 'Perform' the dialogue as they write; revise and refine it.

Whole class

Ask groups of children to perform their play/filmscripts. How have they changed the written version? Why? Discuss the different ways in which the same episode has been treated.

Watch the film/TV episode from Lesson 1 again. Discuss and evaluate the use of dialogue in this episode.

Theme 8) Shakespeare

Objectives

Text level:
- 1 to compare and evaluate a play in print and film/TV version
- 4 to be familiar with the work of established authors; know what is special about their work
- 5 to contribute constructively to discussion about literature
- 11 to read and examine biographical texts
- 14 to develop the skills of biographical writing

Sentence level:
- 4 to investigate connecting words and phrases.

Word level:
- 7 to understand how words and expressions have changed over time

Resources

Biographical writing about Shakespeare; copies of scenes from a chosen Shakespeare play (the abridged versions of selected plays by Leon Garfield for the *Animated Shakespeare* are ideal); a film, TV or audio version of these scenes – including the animated versions; a prose version of the play.
Copymasters 15 and 16, Homework 8

Assessment

At the end of this theme is the pupil able to:
- identify and discuss aspects of Shakespeare's life and works;
- understand the features of biographical writing, and use them in their own writing;
- describe examples of language change over time?

Lesson 1

Whole class

Explain that in this unit they will be finding out about the life and work of William Shakespeare. Ask the children in pairs to share what they know about Shakespeare; then pool ideas as a class and record key facts on the board.
Read children a brief extract from a biography of Shakespeare. Ask children what kind of text this is, and how they can tell. Introduce or revise characteristic features of biographical writing. Write a list of temporal connectives used; identify their function; add other examples to the list. Ask children to distinguish between examples of fact and opinion in the text read.
With the children, identify aspects of Shakespeare's life and works that they would like to find out more about. Record these in the first two columns of a KWL grid (what we Know; what we Want to find out). Organise groups and/or individuals to research these questions.

Group and independent work

Children use non-fiction sources to find answers to the questions they have raised. They then write extended answers to these questions, using, wherever appropriate, the biographical form.

Differentiation

Low Attainers – Give children simple questions about Shakespeare's life to answer.
High Attainers – Research Shakespeare's work, rather than events in his life.

Whole class

Return to the KWL grid. Choose questions and ask children to read out the answers they have written. Prompt others to consider whether the information really does provide an answer and whether it raises other interesting questions. If answers are in biographical form, identify and discuss features of the genre used, and whether opinions as well as facts are included.

Lesson 2

Whole class

Introduce the chosen play, *e.g. explaining when in Shakespeare's career it was written and providing background information.* Read the prose version of the play to the children, or share the reading with them. Pause from time to time to talk about what has happened and what might happen next; prompt children to focus in on the development of plot and character, the setting or settings, and underlying themes. Then give children a short 'time out' to reflect on the story as a whole; you could write up 'big' questions to prompt this, *e.g. What is the key moment? the turning point?* Then share ideas, encouraging children to respond to and build on each other's contributions. Re-read the episode on which you have chosen to focus. Prompt children to discuss what part this plays in the story as a whole.

Group and independent work

Children read and respond to the story or an extract from it, *e.g. recording events on a time-line, writing a character sketch, planning a tableau presentation, writing a blurb.*

Differentiation

Low Attainers – Read only the focus scene, and respond in visual images, *e.g. drawing a cover picture or cartoon strip version.*
High Attainers – Focus on a main character, and write their 'story', *e.g. retelling an episode from their point of view or as a diary.*

Whole class

Ask children to share independent work relevant to the scene to be studied in the next lesson. Consolidate and extend their understanding of the characters featured, of what happens and how this fits into the story.

Lesson 3

Whole class

Prepare an enlarged text version of all or part of the scene, and copies for individuals or pairs.

Watch and/or listen to a film, television or audio version of this part of the play. Explain that this is a performance of the scene as Shakespeare wrote it. Now read the enlarged text to the children, asking them to follow. Re-read it, this time with the children, giving some of them parts to read. Briefly discuss how this compares with the prose version they read in the previous lesson.

Explain that in this lesson they will be focusing on the language of the play. Ask children: What do you notice? and encourage them to share initial ideas. Prompt them (as appropriate) to identify and discuss examples of imagery; use of prose and/poetry; how the poetry is structured in (generally unrhymed) lines; choice of words. Mark up and annotate the enlarged text.

Group and independent work

Children re-read the scene, on their own or in pairs, making notes about how it is written or annotating their copies of the text.

Differentiation

Low Attainers – Watch the film/TV performance of the scene while following the text.

High Attainers – Suggest a particular language focus, e.g. imagery, choice of vocabulary.

Whole class

Show the enlarged text version of the scene again. Go through it line by line, asking children what they noticed about how it is written. Add to the annotations as appropriate. Encourage children to formulate and share general ideas about the language and style of the scene.

Lesson 4

Whole class

Show and begin reading the enlarged text of the chosen scene. Pause when you reach the first instance of a word or word form (e.g. *makst*) which is no longer in common use. Ask children to comment. Draw out the idea that the English language has changed in many ways since Shakespeare wrote.

Read on together, pausing to identify and discuss other examples of words and expressions that are no longer current. Highlight them in the text and/or write up as a list. Consider how we might say the same thing now. Look for ways of classifying these words, *e.g. old verb endings (makst, doth), old pronouns (thee, thou, thine), words that are rarely used now (hither, yon).*

If there are few such examples in the scene, you could supplement this by reading other extracts together.

Group and independent work

Children read the rest of this scene, or another extract from a Shakespeare play or a poem; find 'old' words and expressions and identify modern forms or equivalents.

Differentiation

Low Attainers – Copymaster 15 – a song

High Attainers – Copymaster 16: read and identify 'old' words in an extract from Henry V.

Whole class

Ask children to contribute old words and expressions that they have found. Record these in two columns headed: Old word and What we would say now. Extend this work by looking together for examples of 'old' grammar and sentence structure.

Lesson 5

Whole class

Show the enlarged text again, and ask children to identify features that show it is a playscript. Draw children's attention to the description of setting at the start of the scene, use of stage directions, characters' names, etc.

Note any differences between this and modern playscripts with which they are familiar (for example, the scene might include a soliloquy or a song).

Show the film/TV version. Discuss how the scene is acted and realised in this performance, considering costume, action and setting. How well does it work? How might it be done differently?

Give the relevant number of experienced readers a copy of the script, and ask them to try an informal performance of the first few exchanges in the scene. Discuss how they could use their voices, gestures and movement to express the characters' feelings and relationships.

Group and independent work

Children work in groups to plan and rehearse an informal performance of the scene. Give one child in each group the role of Director, and ask them to listen and identify strengths and weaknesses. The group then attempts an improved performance.

Differentiation

Organise mixed ability groups, giving high attainers the longer and more challenging parts to read.

Whole class

Ask a group to present their performance of the scene. Ask the other children to comment, identifying first what they did well, and then any problems. Look for opportunities to direct children's attention back to the meaning and language of the scene, *e.g. a character's feelings at that point, the rhythm and phrasing of the poetry.*

Theme 9) Viewpoint in fiction

Objectives

Text level:
- 2 to take account of viewpoint in a novel: identifying narrator; explaining effect; considering other viewpoints
- 3 to articulate personal responses to literature
- 4 to be familiar with the work of established authors
- 6 to manipulate narrative perspective: write in voice of a text; write story with two narrators
- 7 to plan own narrative writing

Sentence level:
- 1 to revise word classes (pronouns); adapting texts for particular purposes

Word level:
- 1 to build spellings by syllabic parts; apply knowledge of spelling rules and exceptions; build words from known words

Resources

A collection of novels and short stories told in the first and third persons, including work by established authors. Look for variety within each of these categories, *e.g. first person narrators who are participants and ones who are onlookers; third person narratives which are 'even-handed' and omniscient and ones which take the viewpoint of a particular character.*
Copymasters 17 and 18, Homework 9

Assessment

At the end of this theme is the pupil able to:
- understand the range of viewpoints from which a narrative can be told, and the different ways in which each influences the reader's response;
- identify and comment on the viewpoint adopted in specific novel, and how this affects the reader;
- make decisions about viewpoint and narrative perspective in their own writing;
- use a range of spelling strategies?

Lesson 1

Whole class

Explain that in this unit the class will be exploring different viewpoints from which stories can be told. Read the beginning of a first-person story. Ask: Whose voice do we hear? How can we tell? Now read an extract from a third-person narrative, and ask the questions again. Establish and revise the basic distinction between first and third person narratives.
Ask children how the first story would be different if told in the third person and the second if told in the first person. Adapt the first few sentences in each extract; focus on change of pronouns.
Discuss the possibilities each 'voice' opens up for the author and the different ways the reader relates to the action.

Group and independent work

Children search the classroom or library collection of fiction, and find one story told in the first person and one in the third. They rewrite the first few sentences of each in the 'other' person.

Differentiation

Low Attainers – Sort four or six given books into the two categories.
High Attainers – Write brief commentaries on the different ways in which the reader sees and responds to the action.

Whole class

Ask children to share opening sentences from stories told in the first person; identify who is telling the story; and comment on the effect. Then present their 're-tellings'. What did they need to change? How is the effect different? Repeat this with opening sentences from stories told in the third person.

Lesson 2

Whole class

Prepare extracts from stories told in the first person: one where the narrator is a major participant; one where he is an onlooker; one where there is more than one narrator. Divide the children into three groups; give pairs of children in each group copies of the same extract to read.
Ask each group to tell the others how their story is told, prompting them to go beyond the fact that it is in the first person: Who is telling the story? What is their role? Their view of events? Consider the different effects created by these ways of telling a story. Choose an episode from a traditional tale. Ask children to retell it in two or three first person versions, each from the point of view of a different character. They could do this orally or in writing. Ask each group to find in their extract a word which follows and a word which breaks a particular spelling rule; share these words; add others which follow/break the rules.

Group and independent work

Assemble a collection of first-person stories. Ask children to read the beginning of one, and to write a label describing who is telling the story and what their role in it is. Then re-tell a moment from a traditional tale told from the point of view of the different characters involved.

Differentiation

Low Attainers – Re-tell episode from a traditional tale from the point of view of the main character.
High Attainers – Include comments on how the narrative perspective affects the reader.

Whole class

Share some of the labels the children have written. Prompt them to consider the effect on the reader. Ask children to read different tellings of the same story. Can the others guess what the story is, and who is telling it?

Lesson 3
Whole class

Prepare enlarged text versions of the openings of two novels or short stories written in the third person: one in which the author writes from inside the mind of a particular character and one in which the author takes a more distant, broad perspective on events and characters and comments on them.

Read the extracts with the children. Confirm that they are both in the third person, but that within this there are differences of perspective. Prompt children to identify and comment on these differences; highlight and annotate relevant sections of the text. Discuss how these different narrative approaches influence the reader's view of events and his/her response.

Ask children to find in the extract a word that includes a prefix or suffix and one which resembles another word in some respect. Share these words; explain the resemblance. List other words with the same structures.

Group and independent work

Assemble a collection of third-person stories. Ask children to read the beginning of one, and to write a label describing how the story is told. If time, they could re-work the first few sentences taking a different third-person approach.

Differentiation

Low Attainers – Give children two books with clearly contrasting approaches.

High Attainers – Include comments on how this third-person perspective affects the reader.

Whole class

Pull together work from Lessons 1, 2 and 3 by working with the children to write a brief description of different narrative perspectives, and to find, from the books read, a clear example of each. Write an illustrative quotation to accompany each description. This could be presented as a poster.

Lesson 4 (including SAT preparation)
Whole class

Re-read one of the enlarged texts from Lesson 3 with the children, extending it if necessary to make a substantial extract.

Formulate questions about it in the various formats used in end of Key Stage 2 English SATs: identifying the right answer from four alternatives; ordering brief descriptions of events in the correct order; explaining the significance of short extracts from the story; finding evidence in the text to support various statements, *e.g. about character and motivation;* answering open questions; answering questions about how the story is written, *e.g. word choice and imagery;* expressing and justifying opinions about the story.

Emphasise the importance of understanding the kind of response required for each format, of really answering the question, and of drawing on information in the text.

Revise appropriate reading strategies for this.

Group and independent work

Children use SAT formats to formulate their own questions about one of the extracts they have been reading in the previous lessons; give questions (and text) to others to answer; and check the answers.

Differentiation

Low Attainers – Copymaster 17. Write two multiple choice questions and two open questions; swap with a partner and try to answer the questions.

High Attainers – Copymaster 18. Write statements about the main character, and back them from the text.

Whole class

Share a question of each type; identify the kind of response required to answer it.

Gauge (from monitoring independent work) the types of question which are proving difficult. Work through more examples of each type.

Lesson 5 (including SAT preparation)
Whole class

Choose an open-ended title for story writing (*e.g. Lost and Found*); to provide more stimulus, relate this to a story read in the previous lessons. Explain that the children are going to write their own story with this title. Give them a few minutes 'time out' to think about their story; they could jot down ideas or begin planning. Briefly share some ideas for stories, and choose one to develop with the class. Talk through the decisions and processes involved. What narrative viewpoint will they adopt? Draw on work in previous lessons to consider the options for this. Experiment with writing alternative opening sentences using different perspectives. How are they going to plan their story? Work through techniques for this, *e.g. sketching out the plot by listing main events in chronological order* (emphasise the importance of doing

this very briefly); planning the various elements of the story (characters, setting, action, mood).

Group and independent work

Children plan and begin writing their own story. To provide practice for SATs, set a time limit, *e.g. 20 minutes of this lesson and 20 minutes at some other time.*

Differentiation

Low Attainers – Give children a story starter to continue.

High Attainers – Set children the target of developing an aspect of their story-writing, *e.g. description of setting, characterisation.*

Whole class

Share work so far; prompt children to consider the full range of story elements (setting, characterisation, action, mood).

Discuss pros and cons of various planning formats.

Theme 10 Biography and autobiography

Objectives

Text level:
- 11 to distinguish between biography and autobiography
- 12 to comment critically on the language, style and success of examples of non-fiction
- 14 to develop skills of biographical and autobiographical writing in role

Sentence level:
- 1 to revise adapting texts for particular readers and purposes; word classes
- 4 to investigate connecting words and phrases

Word level:
- 8 to research the origins of proper names (family names)

Resources
Biographies and autobiographies, linked where possible to work in other areas of the curriculum; enlarged text versions of extracts from biography and autobiography; a variety of other biographical and autobiographical forms, e.g. CVs, reports, obituaries; dictionaries and reference books explaining the origins of family names. Copymasters 19 and 20, Homework 10

Assessment
At the end of this theme is the pupil able to:
- distinguish between biography and autobiography;
- identify and comment on issues in biographical and autobiographical writing, e.g. *fact and opinion, implicit and explicit viewpoints;*
- write in a variety of biographical and autobiographical forms, using the characteristic features of the genres effectively;
- identify some of the origins of family names?

Lesson 1

Whole class

Read aloud an extract from an autobiography about someone the children are familiar with. Ask them what kind of writing this is and what they notice. Draw out the idea that it is a non-fiction text; that its subject matter is the life of a particular person; that it is usually organised chronologically. Identify the words that indicate chronological sequencing of events.

Read an extract from an biography, and ask the children to compare this with the previous text. Point out that here the subject is writing about him or herself; note the use of first person pronouns.

Introduce and explain the terms biography and autobiography to describe these text types. The etymology of the words makes their meanings clear: bio (life), graphy (writing), auto (self).

Write up a couple of sentences about your own life; ask children to rework them as biography.

Group and independent work
Children search collections to find examples of biographical and autobiographical writing; read a few pages from each, and be ready to share ideas about them. Then write about a memorable episode in their own lives, first as autobiography, then as biography.

Differentiation
Low Attainers – Copymaster 19. Read short biographical and autobiographical texts; sort them into sets.
High Attainers – Note differences and similarities between the texts they have found.

Whole class
Ask children to share examples of the biographical and autobiographical texts they have found; develop the discussion of the features of each. Share matching pairs of autobiographical and biographical writing. Discuss what is involved in changing from one to the other.

Lesson 2

Whole class

Read the enlarged text version of a passage of biographical writing with the children. Discuss sources the author might have drawn on and what his/her attitude to the subject seems to be. Ask them to re-read the extract independently, looking in particular for examples of fact and opinion, and any evidence of the author's personal viewpoint and whether this is explicit or implicit. Ask pairs of children to share ideas about these issues; then pool them as a class. Highlight these features on the text.

Introduce and explain other forms of biographical writing, e.g. *(school) reports, obituaries, descriptions in Missing Persons or Wanted notices.* If possible show examples. Use shared writing techniques to compose a school report about an imagined child. Then for the same child, write the text for a Missing Persons notice.

Discuss how the text needs to be adapted for this different purpose.

Group and independent work
Use one of the biographical forms discussed in whole-class work to write about themselves (in the third person), about a friend, or about a favourite character in fiction.

Differentiation
Low Attainers – Provide a framework of headings to support the writing.
High Attainers – Read an extract from a biography; make notes about the issues discussed.

Whole class
Ask children to introduce and read their biographical writing, explaining what form it takes but not revealing the identity of the subject. Can the others guess who it is? What words provide strongest clues? What class are they? Ask children who have been reading other biographical texts to share what they have found out.

Lesson 3

Whole class

Read the enlarged text version of a passage of autobiographical writing with the children. Extend the discussion of how this differs from biography. Draw their attention in particular to the different sources of information (the subject/author knows the experiences from the 'inside'); to the issue of objectivity (can the reader assume that the information is accurate?); to the effect on the reader.

Introduce and explain the CV as another form of autobiographical writing; describe and demonstrate the different ways in which CVs can be organised (*e.g. chronological record starting in present or past; or describing the subject's skills and experiences*).

Choose one of these forms, and use shared writing techniques to compose a CV for a child in the class or a familiar character in fiction.

Group and independent work

Children write a CV in one of the forms discussed about themselves or 'in role' as a famous person in history or a celebrity. If they are writing about themselves, suggest jobs for which they might (fancifully) be applying, *e.g. member of a Premier League football team or the cast of a TV soap opera.*

Differentiation

Low Attainers – Write a CV under given headings, *e.g. school, hobbies, sports.*

High Attainers – Copymaster 20. Complete pro forma for a non-chronological CV applying for a particular job.

Whole class

Ask children who have written CVs in application for the same job to read them out; ask the others to decide who gets the job – and to explain why, referring to information and style: what are the telling words? What class do they belong to?

Lesson 4

Whole class

Explain that in this lesson they will be exploring the origins of surnames. Ask them if they have any thoughts about this. Write up a list of the surnames of people that have featured in the previous lessons (class members, characters in fiction, famous people). Draw their attention to any names in the list that belong to four major sources of surnames: occupations (Smith, Shepherd, Carpenter, Potter, Baker ...); places (Atwood, Bywater, Ford, Church, Hill ...); appearance or character (Short, Longman, Jolly, Armstrong ...); parentage (Johnson, McIntyre, O'Brien, Fitzgerald ...)

Write up these four categories as headings, and (where possible) write listed names under the appropriate one. Brainstorm and record other surnames for each category. Consider names that do not fall into any of these categories. What might their origin be? Can they see any other categories?

Group and independent work

Organise children for the following activities: Read class registers and compile longer lists of surnames for the four main categories; use reference books to research origins of other names; write entries for a dictionary of surnames.

Differentiation

Low Attainers – Sort prepared list of names into the four categories.

High Attainers – Challenge children to find other categories, or to invent new names which belong to the four categories investigated.

Whole class

Ask children to share other names they have found that belong to the four main categories, explaining their original meaning; to suggest other possible categories and names that belong to them; share entries for a dictionary of surnames, and suggest ways in which this might be developed (*e.g. a Year or school dictionary*).

Lesson 5

Whole class

Select someone the children have been studying, *e.g. in History or Art.* Brainstorm facts about their life, or a particular period or episode in it; record these in note form on the board. Use shared writing techniques to begin drafting a biography. Identify and discuss use of connecting words to turn notes into a coherent account. Draw children's attention to the issues discussed in Lesson 2: fact, opinion, fiction, viewpoint (explicit and implicit).

Now invite the children to take on the role of the person in question. How could the first few sentences of the biography be reworked as autobiography? Draw their attention to issues discussed in Lesson 3. What information could they add? (Prompt them to imagine themselves into the person's thoughts and feelings.) Is there anything they would need to change or remove? Work together to compose an autobiographical version.

Group and independent work

Children research the life of a person of their own choice, drawing on a range of sources (not just biographies or autobiographies), and present it either as a biography or an autobiography. This provides a context for extended writing.

Differentiation

Low Attainers – Focus on just one episode in or period of the person's life.

High Attainers – Write a biography; include not only facts but also opinions about the person's work and/or importance.

Whole class

Share work in progress. Prompt children to discuss and evaluate not only the content of the writing, but also the extent to which it follows the conventions of the chosen text type, raising issues discussed in the unit.

Theme 1) Word roots and origins

Objectives

Word level:

- 2 to use known spellings as a basis for spelling other words with related patterns or similar meanings
- 3 to build up spellings using known prefixes, suffixes and letter strings; apply knowledge of spellings and rules and exceptions; build words from other known words and from awareness of the meaning or derivations of words
- 5 to extend work on word origins and derivations

Resources

A variety of sophisticated dictionaries, including ones providing information on etymology. An enlarged version of a text with challenging vocabulary and some words with irregular spellings.
Copymasters 21 and 22, Homework 11

Assessment

At the end of this theme is the pupil able to:
- analyse the structure of complex words, showing knowledge of derivations and origins;
- use knowledge of word roots, prefixes and suffixes to spell words;
- apply knowledge of spelling rules and exceptions to spell words?

Lesson 1

Whole class

Explain that they will be investigating the structure and spelling of related words and finding out about their origins. In this lesson the focus is on suffixes that 'mark' nouns.

Write up (or highlight in a text) nouns that end with suffixes, *e.g. punishment, pollution, traveller, exploration, guidance, flexibility, discussion.* Ask children what they notice: draw out the idea that they are all nouns and all end with a suffix.

Give children a few minutes to work individually or in pairs to record the root of each word, what word class it belongs to, and another word ending with the same suffix. Work through one example together, *e.g. possess; noun, possession.* Share and check.

Reorganise and ask pairs or small groups to list ten words ending with one of the noun suffixes. Then ask them to identify cases where they need to change the spelling of the root word before adding the suffix. Draw out related spelling rules, *e.g. dropping final e (guidance), changing y to i (flexibility), doubling final consonant (traveller).*

Group and independent work

Design and write a poster explaining how nouns are formed from other words by the addition of suffixes, illustrating this with examples.

Differentiation

Low Attainers – Focus on suffixes that indicate the performer of an action, *e.g. er, ist, ician.*
High Attainers – Include in their poster an explanation of the spelling rules.

Whole class

Ask children to present work on suffixes that indicate the performer of an action.
Share one or two posters; discuss how clearly and fully they present the information.
Give children a word; ask them to write down the related noun.

Lesson 2

Whole class

In this lesson the focus is on suffixes that 'mark' adjectives. Ask each child to write down on their whiteboard ten adjectives. Ask them what they notice about how these words end. Share suffixes; compile a list of words ending in each. Be ready to contribute additional suffixes, so that common ones are covered (*e.g. tasty, foolish, dangerous, breakable, angelic, creative, musical, obedient, hesitant*).

As in Lesson 1, underline root words and note their word class. Identify patterns, *e.g. ous turns nouns into adjectives; able turns verbs into adjectives.*

Ask children to scan these lists for words where the spelling rules identified in the previous lesson apply. Give pairs a dictionary. Talk through and demonstrate the process of looking up words (nouns and adjectives) that end with suffixes, explaining that this often involves locating the root word and then finding the list of words derived from it. Work through the process a few times with given words.

Group and independent work

Children write (silly) sentences including as many examples as possible of words derived from the same root by the addition of suffixes, *e.g. Marvo the Magical Magician was no good at magic.* Use a dictionary to check spellings.

Differentiation

Low Attainers – Copymaster 21. Cut out and sort 'families' of derived words; use in sentences.
High Attainers – Identify and mark the word class of each word.

Whole class

Share sentences; identify word class of root word and words derived from it; note application of spelling rules.
Give children a word; ask them to write down the related adjective.

Lesson 3

Whole class

In this lesson the focus is on prefixes. Prepare a set of cards with prefixes and root words that can be matched flexibly to form derived words (*e.g. Re, ex, im and trans can be added to port and pose*). Include less common prefixes, *e.g. pro, com, con, ab*. Display on a board. Challenge children to make as many words as they can in two minutes.
Ask for contributions; arrange and rearrange the cards to make the suggested words.
Make a set of words with the same prefix; ask children to work out its meaning.
Write up a list of words that can be given a negative meaning by the addition of different prefixes, *e.g. possible, credible, believable, responsible, obedient, legal*. Add the appropriate prefix to each.
Ask children to list other negative words that begin with each of these prefixes. Identify patterns, *e.g. ir before words beginning with r; im before words beginning with p.*

Group and independent work

Draw together work from Lessons 1–3 by using web diagrams to record words that can be derived from root words by adding prefixes and/or suffixes; note the word class of each.

Differentiation

Low Attainers – Complete a chart with columns root; prefix + root; root + suffix.
High Attainers – Read a text; identify every derived word; write down the root.

Whole class

Share word charts and web diagrams. Identify words that have both prefixes and suffices, or more than one suffix, *e.g. magnificently.*
Ask children who replaced derived with root words in a text to report on what they noticed. What kinds of words were left?

Lesson 4

Whole class

In this lesson the focus is on 'borrowed' words. Recap work in Term 1 on Latin and Greek roots and prefixes. List words including some of them.
Write up a few borrowed words with unusual spellings (select from Copymaster 22).
Ask children what they notice. Identify and discuss unusual spelling patterns, *e.g. unusual relationships between letters/letter strings and phonemes, breaking of rules (e.g. words ending k rather than ck).*
Explain that these words have come into English from other languages, and that this is an important aspect of the growth of the language. Discuss how and why this happens, *e.g. through cultural contact; to name objects newly encountered (e.g. tobacco).*
Revise use of etymological and other dictionaries to find out about word origins.

Organise the class into groups to look up five 'borrowed' words; share findings.

Group and independent work

Use a dictionary which provides information about the origin of words. Assign groups a letter of the alphabet, and ask them to look for words with interesting origins.

Differentiation

Low Attainers – Give children a list of words with the same language of origin to look up
High Attainers – Copymaster 22. Use a dictionary to find the origins of given words; identify and explain what is unusual about the spelling of each.

Whole class

Ask children to contribute words originating from particular languages/countries. Note any patterns, *e.g. Italian words to do with music and food.* Note any unusual spellings. Display a large map of the world. Organise children to pin words to places of origin.

Lesson 5

Whole class

In this lesson the focus is on irregular words and on spelling rules and exceptions to them.
Read the enlarged text together. Ask them to find:
• words that follow a spelling rule. Share these; prompt children to explain each rule, to list other words that follow it and any that are exceptions;
• words that are exceptions to a spelling rule; explain what the rule is and list words that do follow it;
• words that have irregular spelling patterns; identify what is unusual about them;
• the word that is most difficult to spell; identify and discuss what makes it difficult.
Share ideas on this. Explain that different people find different kinds of words tricky.

Group and independent work

Carry out the same procedure with another text, recording words of these kinds. Use this as the starting point for reflecting on their own progress in spelling, noting strengths and weaknesses (*e.g. in columns with these headings*).

Differentiation

Low Attainers – Review recent marked writing; identify 'difficult' words they got right; identify patterns in errors, and record them, *e.g. in a sentence beginning 'I often have trouble words that…'*
High Attainers – In addition, develop an action plan to improve their spelling.

Whole class

Ask some children to share their strengths and weaknesses as spellers. Discuss and plan strategies for improving spelling, *e.g. by keeping individual spelling logs.*

Theme 2) Commentaries and summaries

Objectives

NOTE This theme is designed for use in preparation for the Key Stage 2 English SAT for Reading.

Text level:
- 8 to analyse the success of texts
- 14 to write commentaries or summaries.

Sentence level:
- 3 to revise work on complex sentences
- to revise work on contracting sentences (summary, note making)

Word level:
- 2 to use known spellings as a basis for spelling other words
- 3 to use independent spelling strategies

Resources

A relatively challenging extract from fiction and non-fiction, some or all presented as an enlarged text. Copymasters 23 and 24, Homework 12

Assessment

At the end of this theme is the pupil able to:
- understand and respond to fiction and non-fiction texts, referring to the text to support their answers and views;
- write commentaries on the qualities and effectiveness of texts;
- summarise a text, identifying key points;
- use knowledge of sophisticated spelling patterns and word derivation to analyse the structure of words and to support their spelling?

Lesson 1

Whole class

Explain that in this theme they will explore two texts in detail, and prepare for tests in reading.

Read the fiction extract with the children, presenting all or some of it as an enlarged text. Ask two questions: one requiring recall of simple factual information; the other requiring inference or deduction. Share answers, referring to relevant parts of the text.

Ask children to pose their own questions; share and answer some. Talk through the process of searching the text, expressing the answer clearly, and checking that it matches the question.

Explain the question formats used in the fiction part of reading SATs. Distinguish between those with one right answer and those with a range of acceptable answers which they need to justify by reference to the text.

Write up a word from the text; ask children to jot down

words that are related to it in some way, *e.g. same letter string, same rule, same root, prefix or suffix.* Share words, explaining the relationship.

Group and independent work

Write up a list of other words for the children to analyse and explore as in whole-class work. Use a web diagram, with the target word in the centre, to record this.

Differentiation

Low Attainers – Copymaster 23. List related words with given properties.

High Attainers – Challenge children to find as many different kinds of relationships as they can.

Whole class

Choose one of the words. Work together to pool and record related words, exploring this in as many ways as possible. Explain how they can use knowledge of known words to help them spell other words that are related to them.

Lesson 2

Whole class

Re-read the fiction text. Explain that now they are going to explore how it is written and the effect it creates. Ask children to re-read independently, and then share ideas with a partner.

Lead a whole-class discussion. Prompt children to focus on significant issues, *e.g. description of character and setting, suspense, dialogue, genre features,* and to refer to the detail of the text. List key ideas, and/or annotate the text.

Work through SAT questions which focus on language; apply them, where possible, to this text, and develop full and accurate answers.

Introduce and explain the term 'commentary'. Model how to plan a commentary, drawing on earlier discussion, and work together to write one section. Emphasise the importance of referring to the text and the author, *e.g. the author describes the setting very vividly by . . .*

Ask: What do you think is the most difficult word in the

extract to spell? Why? Share ideas, focusing on irregular spellings and exceptions to rules.

Group and independent work

Children write their own commentary on the fiction extract read or another of their own choice. Write up a list of headings to help them focus and structure their work.

Differentiation

Low Attainers – Write answers to SAT format questions about the extract.

High Attainers – Write a detailed commentary on one or two striking aspects of the text.

Whole class

Monitor independent work, and choose paragraphs which illustrate the content and style of commentaries. Present these to the class, using them to reinforce and extend the key teaching points.

Lesson 3

Whole class

Read the non-fiction extract with the children, presenting all or some of it as an enlarged text. Ask two questions: one requiring recall of simple factual information; the other requiring children to make inferences or deduction or to draw together information from different parts of the text. Share and check answers.

As in Lesson 1, ask children to pose and answer their own questions, referring to the text, and checking that they really have answered the question.

Ask and answer questions about how the information is presented.

Demonstrate and explain the question formats they are likely to meet in the non-fiction part of reading SATs. Work through the text, prompting children to describe the structure of each sentence, *e.g. identifying the main*

clause, connecting words, passive/active constructions, and how punctuation is used to demarcate grammatical boundaries.

Group and independent work

Prepare a Find A Sentence task board which prompts children to look for sentences with particular features, *e.g. includes a connecting word, in the passive, with just one clause.* Children search a non-fiction text for sentences which exemplify these features, and write them down.

Differentiation

Low Attainers – Use a simplified version of the task board to find a limited range of features.
High Attainers – Copymaster 24. Read sophisticated information text; annotate it to show structure of sentences.

Whole class

Choose one of the features on the task board, and ask children to share sentences which exemplify. Check and confirm. Repeat with other features.

Lesson 4

Whole class

Re-read the non-fiction extract. Give children a couple of minutes to list five main points, individually or with a partner. Share, and agree on these points. Highlight them in the text, *e.g. by underlining key words.*

Discuss and experiment with ways of re-presenting the information in the extract graphically, *e.g. as an annotated time-line, diagram, flow-chart.* Decide on what would be appropriate for this information.

Introduce and explain the idea of writing a summary. Use shared writing techniques to compose a summary of the extract in prose form (rather than notes), drawing on earlier work in the lesson.

As the writing proceeds look for opportunities to revise work on contracting sentences, *e.g. removing unnecessary words; combining sentences to avoid repetition.*

Group and independent work

Children write a prose summary of this extract or of the non-fiction text they worked with in Lesson 3. About five minutes before the end of this session, ask them to check whether they can contract any sentences.

Differentiation

Low Attainers – Develop whole-class work to re-present the information graphically, with accompanying annotation, working on large sheets of paper.
High Attainers – Set a maximum word limit for their summary.

Whole class

Help children to present graphical representations of the information; discuss effectiveness of these: what is clearer? less clear?

Share and compare two or three summaries of the same text. Which is shortest? Does it miss out anything important?

Lesson 5

Whole class

Prepare for this lesson by choosing a commentary and a summary which are interesting and/or problematic. With their authors' permission, share these with the class, if possible presenting them as enlarged texts. Read the commentary together. Discuss and evaluate with the children: Does it really comment, or just describe? Does it refer to the author and to the text? Annotate the text to show ways of improving it, and revise.

Read the summary together. Ask the children if they can see any ways in which the text could be shortened, either by deleting information which is not essential, or by contracting sentences. Experiment with ways of doing this, and revise as appropriate.

Draw together the work on SATs, by reviewing the range of question formats, and stressing the key strategies, *e.g. finding the answer in the text, reading the question carefully, checking you have answered it.*

Group and independent work

Children choose a fiction or non-fiction extract, and devise their own SAT test on it, using a range of question formats; keep a record of right (or acceptable) answers or 'mark scheme'. Write up 'blank' formats as a reminder of the different formats.

Differentiation

Low Attainers – Write questions for one of the texts explored in whole-class work.
High Attainers – Challenge children to include a question of every type.

Whole class

Ask children to contribute a question in a particular format; share any issues or problems raised. Repeat with other formats. (Make time available for children to answer each other's questions, and for the 'setters' to mark them.)

Theme 3) Genres in fiction

Objectives

Text level:
- 7 to identify key features of different types of literary texts
- 8 to analyse the success of texts and writers in achieving effects
- 10 to use different genres as models for own writing
- 12 to study in depth one genre and produce an extended piece of similar writing
- 13 to parody a literary text

Word level:
- 2 to use independent spelling strategies
- 4 to learn and invent spelling rules and mnemonics

Resources

Collections of books representing different genres of fiction: thrillers (e.g. 'Goosebumps' series, Joan Aiken short stories); science fiction and fantasy worlds (e.g. Nicholas Fisk, Robert Leeson's 'Zarnia Experiment' series); historical (e.g. Leon Garfield, Adele Geras, Jill Paton Walsh); parodies (e.g. Jon Scieszka's 'Time Warp Trio' series; Alan Coren's 'Arthur' stories). Enlarged text versions of extracts illustrating the features of each of these genres. Work on this unit should come towards the end of the term when children have read widely and independently in these genres.
Copymasters 25 and 26, Homework 13

Assessment

At the end of this theme is the pupil able to:
- identify the literary genre to which particular novels and short stories belong;
- identify and discuss the characteristic features of these genres, in terms of plot, character and language;
- write a story using the features of one of these genres;
- identify and write literary parodies;
- identify patterns in spelling and word structure?

Lesson 1

Whole class

Explain that in this theme they will be looking at different kinds of fiction. Read aloud an extract from a thriller. Ask children what kind of story this is and how they can tell; introduce and explain the term. Display and read an enlarged text of some of this extract. Identify and discuss in more detail the characteristic features of the genre, focusing on action, suspense, and style. Mark up and annotate the text; write a list of features for display. Discuss how effectively the author has created the desired effect.
Prompt children to tell the class about other books of this kind that they have read, what features of the genre they use, and how effective they are.
Ask children to find in the text words that include prefixes and/or suffixes; write them down; draw vertical lines to show the structure of the word. Share; ask children to explain how the prefix or suffix alters the root word.

Group and independent work

Give groups a thriller, with a marked passage. Ask children to read this together; to note features of the genre; and to discuss how well it works. Make notes on this, and prepare a reading aloud performance. Identify and list words with prefixes/suffixes.

Differentiation

Low Attainers – Copymaster 25. Underline prefix/suffix in words; write other words beginning/ending with them.
High Attainers – Copymaster 26. Use chart to analyse words with both prefixes and suffixes.

Whole class

Ask groups to introduce, comment on and read aloud the passage they have worked on. Add to or develop the list of features. Share words with interesting structures of prefixes/suffixes.

Lesson 2

Whole class

Read aloud a descriptive passage from a science fiction or fantasy novel. Ask children to sketch what they see in their mind's eye. Then share and compare sketches with a partner.
Read together an enlarged text version of this extract. Ask again: What kind of story is this? How can we tell? Confirm terminology. Identify features of the genre; prompt children to draw more widely on their reading to add to and develop these ideas. Write a list of characteristic features under headings for plot, setting, character, language. Underline words and phrases that describe the new world and/or creatures. Discuss how effectively he/she has realised this. Is it convincing?
Ask children to find in the text words with 1, 2, 3 ... syllables. Share; identify word with most syllables.

Group and independent work

Give children a copy of the same (unillustrated) descriptive passage. Ask them to respond to this visually, *e.g. drawing the text illustration, designing and illustrating the book cover or film poster.* Prompt them to refer to the text.

Differentiation

Low Attainers – Give children just a few vivid lines from the extract to present as a page from a picture book.
High Attainers – Add labels and notes to the picture indicating aspects that cannot easily be shown.

Whole class

Give children a few minutes to compare their visual representations. Show the enlarged text again. Share ideas: what elements of the text have they used? What is difficult/impossible to show? Refer back to the detail of the text.

Lesson 3

Whole class

(Before the lesson, ask children to select an extract from an historical novel.)

Ask two or three to read aloud extracts from novels set in the same period. Ask the others to identify this period, and how they knew.

Read together an enlarged version of an extract from a novel in which historical background is prominent. Give children a couple of minutes to jot down what they learn about the period. Share ideas. Discuss whether the description is accurate and realistic, drawing on their knowledge of the period. Highlight parts of the text which convey the historical background, drawing attention to description of settings, the way people talk, events and themes.

Ask children to find in the text a word that is tricky to spell. Share; explain why; invent a rule or mnemonic that helps with this spelling.

Group and independent work

Groups choose a simple event, *e.g. going shopping, being late for school;* each member of the group writes a short narrative account, setting the event in a particular period. Ask some groups to work on large sheets of paper which can be displayed.

Differentiation

Low Attainers – Children write an extended caption for a picture of an historical scene.

High Attainers – Give children a list of elements to include in their account, *e.g. action, dialogue, description of character and setting.*

Whole class

Ask one group to display and read their narratives; ask others to identify the periods, and aspects of the text which established this. Highlight these; if time allows, discuss ways of developing the text.

Lesson 4

Whole class

Read an enlarged text extract from a novel which parodies one of the genres discussed in Lesson 1 or 2. Ask: What do you notice? How can we tell it is making fun of a kind of writing? Introduce and explain the term parody. Discuss examples of parody from film and television – which may well be more familiar than ones from fiction. Re-read the enlarged text. Prompt children to identify how the effect is achieved, looking in particular at the exaggeration of genre features (setting, action, characters, language).

Choose another fiction genre. Recap its features, and discuss how you could parody it. Plan an opening sequence for such a parody, and write the first few sentences together.

Return to the enlarged text. Ask children to find and list words with a particular long vowel phoneme. Share;

identify different ways of spelling this phoneme; list other words that follow each pattern.

Group and independent work

Children write a short episode parodying one of the genres they have been studying. Display lists of characteristic features compiled in previous lessons for children to refer to.

Differentiation

Low Attainers – Depending on the chosen genre, write only a description of setting, action or character.

High Attainers – Write a parody of one of the extracts studied in Lesson 1 or 2.

Whole class

Choose a genre. Ask a pair of children to read extracts from the 'real thing' and a parody of it which they have written. Which is which? How can you tell? Repeat with another genre.

Lesson 5

Whole class

Choose a genre studied in the first three lessons. Display and review the list of features. Give pairs of children a few minutes to invent an opening for a story in this genre. Where might the story begin? What characters might we meet? How might the action start? Share ideas; choose an episode to develop together. Plan the episode in more detail, considering setting, character and plot. Use shared writing strategies to draft the opening paragraphs of the story. Draw children's attention to the language of the genre, for example by re-reading the relevant enlarged text extract. Read the draft together. Identify ways in which the characteristic features of the genre could be used more fully. Revise and improve.

Group and independent work

Children choose a genre to work in, and plan an opening episode for a story using the strategy from the whole-class phase. Then write the episode. This provides a context for extended writing in other literacy hours, when you could extend knowledge of the genre conventions, and other aspects of narrative writing.

Differentiation

Low Attainers – Base their story on an episode studied in the theme, *e.g. by continuing it or changing an element.*

High Attainers – Give children opportunities to develop and revise their writing to presentation standard.

Whole class

Share work in progress by displaying plans and opening paragraphs; give children time to read some of these and to share comments on them. Lead this discussion, developing their understanding of the conventions of the genres.

Theme 4) Humorous verse

Objectives

Text level:

- 3 to recognise how poets manipulate words
- 4 to investigate humorous verse
- 9 to increase familiarity with work of significant poets of the past
- 10 to use different genres as models for own writing

Word level:

- 2 to use known spellings as basis for spelling other words

Resources

Collections of humorous verse, including examples from the past (especially Lewis Carroll, Edward Lear and Hilaire Belloc) and the present (Spike Milligan, Shel Silverstein, William Cole) and covering the range noted in lessons below. Enlarged text versions of poems of these kinds.
Copymasters 27 and 28, Homework 14

Assessment

At the end of this theme is the pupil able to:

- describe and comment on features of different kinds of humorous verse;
- identify and explain examples of language play, including nonsense verse and invented words;
- use humorous poems read as basis for writing their own in the same form;
- invent new words following known spelling patterns and word structures?

Lesson 1

Whole class

Explain that in this theme the children will be exploring different kinds of humorous poetry and language play. Read one of the longer, narrative nonsense poems by Lewis Carroll or Edward Lear aloud to the class, or ask children to do so, sharing verses. Ask children to retell the story together – a sentence each.

Display an enlarged text version of some or all the poem. Prompt children to share ideas about the humour and appeal of the poem; focus their attention on the 'nonsense' elements, and introduce this term. Look more closely at where the nonsense lies (*e.g. in characters, setting, action*) and how it works (*e.g. through impossibilities, reversals, comic juxtapositions*). Focus on the language of the poem, identifying examples of language play and any invented words or names. Note words that follow similar spelling patterns.

Group and independent work

Children search collections of humorous verse for nonsense poems. Choose and write down their favourite lines. Make notes in preparation for introducing and presenting their poem to the class. If working in groups, experiment with possibilities for 'choral reading'.

Differentiation

Low Attainers – Work with a given nonsense poem, with clear and accessible nonsense features.
High Attainers – Write a short (say, two-sentence) review of the poem.

Whole class

Ask selected individuals/groups to introduce and present their nonsense poems. Develop discussion of how poems of this kind work and their appeal, focusing on issues from whole-class work.

Lesson 2

Whole class

Choose a nonsense poem which includes a large number of invented words; Lewis Carroll's 'Jabberwocky' would be ideal. Read an enlarged text version of the poem with the children. Re-tell what happens or describe what the poem is about. Discuss how the reader knows this even though there are lots of 'nonsense' words. Identify and list these words. For each, work out: the part of speech (How do we know this?); a likely meaning, drawing on the sound of the word, its context in the poem, and similarities with other (real) words. Focus on the spelling of the invented words. Explain that, to be pronounceable, invented words have to follow the patterns of English spelling. Emphasise this by writing unpronounceable 'words' that do not follow these patterns, *e.g. hsuogw.*
Identify the patterns and letters strings in each invented word; list other words which follow them.
Write up real words of increasing complexity, *e.g. bed,* table, different, vocabulary. Ask children to invent and jot down an invented words based on each of these structures. Share.

Group and independent work

Children create more invented words, *e.g. based on those in the poem or on a group of thematically related words.* Decide what they mean, and write dictionary definitions.

Differentiation

Low Attainers – Copymaster 27. Distinguish between 'possible' and 'impossible' invented words; invent more based on the possible ones.
High Attainers – Include in their dictionary entry a sentence illustrating the use of the invented word.

Whole class

Children contribute their invented words, orally; work together to spell them, noting range of possible spellings, and consider plausible meanings.

Lesson 3

Whole class

Read examples of limericks by Edward Lear and other poets, including modern ones. Encourage children to read and re-read aloud to get the characteristic rhythm. Discuss the appeal of this kind of humorous verse, noting the catchy rhythm and rhyme; the predictable format of the first line; the element of nonsense; the satisfying surprise or twist in the last line.

Identify and discuss how the poem is organised in lines, and the strict pattern of rhythm and rhyme.

Used shared writing strategies to compose a new second line; a new final line; examples of typical opening lines.

List the rhyming words in each limerick. Extend by adding other words that rhyme; note, where appropriate, different ways in which the same sound can be spelled, *e.g. hate, eight.*

Group and independent work

Children write their own limericks. They could write adaptations of those read, or add more lines to those invented. Support this by displaying a list of place names that are easy to find rhymes for.

Differentiation

Low Attainers – Give children opening lines, or copies of limericks with gaps to fill.
High Attainers – Challenge children to follow the rules for rhyme and rhythm exactly.

Whole class

Ask some children to share their limericks. Identify where they do and do not follow the rules. Discuss which one works best, referring to features identified in whole-class work.

Lesson 4

Whole class

Ask children some prose riddles of the kind found in Christmas crackers; invite them to contribute their own. Discuss how they work.

Explain that riddles are also an old form of poetry. Display and read enlarged text examples of sophisticated, traditional and new riddles, if necessary concealing the answers. Work out the answers, providing additional clues if needed.

Discuss the appeal of riddles of this kind; note the puzzle element and any recurring structures, *e.g. lists of attributes, comparisons ('as X as a Y')*. Draw attention to the metaphorical thinking behind riddles of this kind: an object is seen and described in terms of something else. Work together to invent a new riddle: decide on an object; identify parts or aspects of it; think about these metaphorically (its X is like …); draw on this to write a list of descriptions that hide but provide clues to the identify of the object.

Group and independent work

Children write a riddle of their own, following the process used in whole class work. This works well as a group activity in which each member contributes a clue.

Differentiation

Low Attainers – Write question and answer riddles: Why is an X like a Y? Because …
High Attainers – Copymaster 28. Work out answers to three riddles; use as models for writing own riddles.

Whole class

Children say their riddles; the others try to work out what it is. Identify and discuss how the clues work and how effective they are. Make comparisons with examples read.

Lesson 5

Whole class

Read one of Hilaire Belloc's 'cautionary verses' to the class; pause to discuss and predict the plot, especially before the usually gruesome come-uppance.

Discuss the appeal of this kind of poem: Do they find it funny? Why or why not? What stops it being moving or tragic? (Look at choice of words, use of exaggeration, and rhythm.) What was the purpose of this kind of humorous verse? Identify the general features and typical storyline.

Identify and discuss the structure of the poem, considering organisation in lines and verses, rhyme and rhythm. How do these contribute to the humorous effect? Read the openings of other cautionary verses; ask children to predict how they end. Read the final episodes to check. Develop discussion of the features of this genre. Work together to develop a plot for a modern cautionary tale, identifying the main character, his/her particular kind of misbehaviour, how things get worse and worse, how the character gets his/her 'just reward'. Invent a name for the character and a title for the poem.

Group and independent work

Children use a known technique to plan a cautionary tale, and write it as a prose narrative. Or write an additional episode or new ending for the poem read.

Differentiation

Low Attainers – Write the story planned in whole-class work.
High Attainers – Challenge children to write in verse, using the poem read as a model.

Whole class

Share openings to cautionary tales. Ask others to predict what happens in the end and the moral it illustrates. Discuss whether and how a comic effect has been achieved.

Theme 5) Narrative structure

Objectives

Text level:

- 1 to understand aspects of narrative structure
- 2 to analyse how paragraphs are structured in writing
- 8 to analyse the success of texts
- 11 to write own story using sophisticated narrative devices

Sentence level:

- 4 to revise work on contracting sentences (summary, note making)

Resources

Novels, short, stories and picture books which use a range of sophisticated narrative structures and devices; enlarged text versions of extracts from these, showing handling of time, shifts in narrative, and organisation of paragraphs.
Copymasters 29 and 30, Homework 15

Assessment

At the end of this theme is the pupil able to:

- identify and discuss how the narrative is structured in a particular story;
- understand a range of sophisticated narrative devices;
- use these devices to write a story with a structure that is not simply chronological;
- contract sentences, identifying key meanings?

Lesson 1

Whole class

Explain that in this theme they will be exploring the different ways in which writers indicate and structure time in stories.

Choose a novel with which the children are familiar; if possible, distribute copies. Give them a few minutes to recall the key events of the first chapter, and to compose (orally or in writing) a sentence which summarises them.

Share, compare and evaluate these sentences. Are they clear and accurate?

If the chapter does not have a title, invent one; if it does, discuss its appropriateness, and invent alternatives.

Repeat for the next two or three chapters.

Show enlarged text with the end of of one chapter and beginning of next; identify and discuss the nature of the link and how it is created, *e.g. cliff-hanger,* marking a shift in place or time, or from the concerns of one character to those of another.

Return to the summary sentences; experiment with contracting them still further.

Group and independent work

Write summary sentences and new titles for the first few chapters of other familiar stories. Choose two consecutive chapters; write out the last and first sentences; write note explaining the link.

Differentiation

Low Attainers – Divide a familiar short story into sections; summarise and title each.
High Attainers – Write summary sentences with a given maximum number of words, *e.g. 12.*

Whole class

Share some summary sentences; rewrite together, clarifying and contracting further. What can be removed? What can be expressed more concisely?

Lesson 2

Whole class

Display an enlarged text version of an extract from a novel or short story consisting of several paragraphs, with little, if any, dialogue. Ask children to read this aloud, taking a paragraph each.

Recap the meaning of the term paragraph. Work through the text paragraph by paragraph, identifying the focus of each; write a 'topic sentence' to summarise this.

Identify and discuss how the sequence of paragraphs is organised, *e.g. it might chart the progression of events in time or follow the development of a character's thoughts and feelings.* Note possibilities not illustrated by the chosen text.

Re-read the text, noting how the author links one paragraph to the next, focusing in particular on the use of pronouns (this, she, the others) and of connecting words and phrases (later, and yet, for a moment).

Underline words and phrases that make the text coherent.

Return to the summary sentences; identify ways of contracting them further without losing the sense.

Group and independent work

Read a passage (again with little or no dialogue) from another novel or short story; write a topic sentence for each paragraph. If using photocopies, underline linking words; otherwise, write a list of these.

Differentiation

Low Attainers – Copymaster 29. Sort paragraphs into the right order; underline linking words.
High Attainers – Write a short commentary on how the paragraphs are sequenced and linked.

Whole class

Read enlarged text of extract in which paragraphing contrasts with that used at start of lesson; identify and discuss how paragraphs are focused, sequenced and linked.

Lesson 3

Whole class

Display an enlarged text version of a passage from a story in which the emphasis is on plot development and in which the author creates suspense. Read it together; quickly identify and record key events in note form, making them as brief as possible.

Discuss how much time passes and how this is shown. Identify and highlight relevant words. Focus on the creation of suspense: How does the author make the reader curious, excited about what is happening and what is going to happen next? How effectively is the effect created?

Explain that usually events in a story follow the actual, chronological sequence of events in time, but that authors also sometimes interrupt or change this order. Identify and explain techniques for this, e.g. *flashbacks, dream sequences, stories within stories.*

Read enlarged text versions of examples of these narrative devices, focusing on passages where the author signals the shift into or out of the normal chronological sequence. Highlight relevant words and phrases.

Group and independent work

Children read a passage from a novel or short story which uses one of the devices above; record the narrative structure diagrammatically or visually; and write an explanatory label.

Differentiation

Low Attainers – Read and analyse a picture book text which uses one of these devices.

High Attainers – Copymaster 30. Read and annotate a passage with sophisticated treatment of time.

Whole class

Ask children to describe and explain the handling of time in the story extract they have been studying; to refer to and quote from the text to show how it works.

Lesson 4

Whole class

Explain that in the following two lessons they will plan and begin writing a story in which events are not arranged simply in the order in which they actually happened.

Choose a short, simple story with which the children are familiar, e.g. *a traditional tale.*

Review techniques for analysing the sequence of events in the story, e.g. *list, story ladder, time-line, flow chart.* Introduce and explain any new ones. Use one (or more) to chart the key events in the story, noting events in as few words as possible.

Prompt children to think about how they could introduce a new element into the story which would change its narrative structure, e.g. *a flashback in which Red Riding Hood or the wolf recalls another occasion when they met; Cinderella's dream about going to the ball.*

Use the chosen plotting technique(s) to plan this new version of the story, e.g. *flow chart with a sideways step; time-line with an interruption keyed into the chronological sequence.*

Group and independent work

Children use one of the techniques explained in whole-class work to plan and make brief notes of a story including a sophisticated narrative device; this could be one of their own invention or an adaptation of a known story. Work on a large sheet.

Differentiation

Low Attainers – Adapt a traditional tale; as modelled in whole class work.

High Attainers – Plan a story which includes more than one narrative device.

Whole class

Ask children to present their plans, explaining what narrative device they are using, and for what purpose.

Lesson 5

Whole class

Return to the plan drawn up in the previous lesson. Focus on that part of the story in which the narrative departs from the chronological ordering of events. Give children a few minutes to develop their ideas about the content of the story at this point. Share ideas. Agree on one to use together and develop it, identifying a section in which they need to move into and out of the flashback, dream, etc.

Use shared writing strategies to compose this part of the story. Focus children's attention on the issues raised in previous lessons: the focusing and organisation of material in paragraphs; ways of linking paragraphs coherently; words that signal the passing of time, and in particular here the interruption of the normal chronological sequence. Consider alternatives; revise and improve this aspect of the text.

Group and independent work

Children write the stories that they planned in Lesson 4, focusing on narrative structure. This activity provides an opportunity for extended writing in other literacy hours and/or outside this context.

Differentiation

Low Attainers – Write only that part of the story where the new element has been added.

High Attainers – Write a paragraph by paragraph plan for parts of the story where narrative structure shifts.

Whole class

Ask children to share work in progress and any difficulties they are having. Consolidate and develop understanding of narrative devices and techniques for handling time. Write up and work together to revise extracts from the children's work.

Theme 6) Official language

Objectives

Text level:
- 17 to read and understand examples of official language and its characteristic features
- 20 to discuss the way Standard English varies in different contexts

Sentence level:
- 1 to investigate further the use of active and passive verbs
- 2 to understand features of formal official language
- 3 to revise work on complex sentences

Resources
A variety of official documents and notices, *e.g. consumer guarantees, by-laws (governing behaviour in public parks),* *official forms, documents and reports.* The Post Office is a good source of these. Enlarged text versions of some of these.
Copymasters 31 and 32, Homework 16

Assessment
At the end of this theme is the pupil able to:
- identify and comment on the language features of formal official writing, at text, sentence and word levels;
- understand why language of this kind is appropriate in this context and for this purpose;
- identify and understand the use of active and passive sentences;
- analyse the structure and punctuation of complex sentences?

Lesson 1

Whole class

Read the children part of an official text using formal language. Ask them what it is and what purpose it serves. Explain that in this theme they will be investigating texts of this kind.
Read the rest of the text with the children. Ask questions to probe their understanding of its content; prompt them to raise their own questions.
Shift focus to the language features of the text. Give children a few minutes time out to share ideas with a partner; prompt them to look at word choice and sentence structure.
Share ideas together as a class. Draw attention to the use of an impersonal style, imperatives, and formal vocabulary. Mark up and annotate the text to show significant features, focusing in particular on sentence structure and punctuation.
Ask children to explain why this kind of language is used in this context (*e.g. it is not a personal communication; it is authoritative*).

Group and independent work
Children read other official, formal texts; then identify and comment on their language features, either by marking up and annotating the text or writing notes.

Differentiation
Low Attainers – Work with a shorter, simpler text; give them a prompt sheet detailing what to look for.
High Attainers – Write an explanatory label for the piece, organised under headings suggested by whole-class work.

Whole class
Ask children to present the official text they have been studying; to explain its content and purpose; and to quote sentences and words which illustrate its language features. Have they found any language features that were not discussed in the whole-class phase?
Ask children to bring in examples of this kind of text for the next lesson.

Lesson 2

Whole class

Display an enlarged text version of an official, formal text which uses a variety of characteristic lay-out devices: numbered or bulleted points, footnotes, headings and sub-headings, brackets, different text styles.
Work through the text, prompting children to identify these features and to explain their functions, focusing on how they guide the reader through the text and indicate the status of different parts of it. Annotate the text. Introduce the relevant terminology.
Give pairs of children a few minutes to share and examine the examples of official texts they have brought in. Ask them to say whether their texts make use of the layout features identified.
Ask them to describe and explain the function of any other devices used in these texts.

Choose a text displayed in the classroom (*e.g. rules, fire drill*), and consider whether any of these devices could be used to make the message more clear and effective.

Group and independent work
Children list and explain the layout devices used in texts they have brought in or in the class collection. They then use one of these devices to rework all or part of a school notice, working on large sheets of paper.

Differentiation
Low Attainers – Rework classroom rules using some of the devices discussed.
High Attainers – Write new school rules using as many of the devices as they can.

Whole class
Ask children to share the texts they have reworked, explaining what layout devices they have used and why.

Lesson 3

Whole class

Choose an official text which makes use of passive constructions. Prepare an enlarged version in which the passive verbs (*e.g. must be worn*) are covered up.
Read through the text with the children; pause at the concealed verbs and ask children to work out what they are (this is likely to involve reading on). Reveal the verbs to confirm the verb form.
Ask children what they notice about the sentences where verbs had been concealed; draw out the idea that they were all passive constructions. Reinforce understanding of this by transforming the sentence into the active; note how new information has to be added to make the agent explicit.
Discuss why sentences of this kind are often used in formal, official texts: the action is more important than the agent; the text addresses all customer users of the park, rather than specific individuals.

Group and independent work

Write matching pairs of active and passive sentences about a range of school activities, *e.g. going to assembly, lunch-boxes, lunch times.*

Differentiation

Low Attainers – Copymaster 31. Transform sentences from passive to active; write three passive sentences.
High Attainers – Use passive sentences in a longer text about one school activity.

Whole class

Ask children to contribute a passive sentence they have written. Write up some of these; identify and underline the verbs, noting common forms, *e.g. been, was, were, are.* Transform the sentence into the active, identifying changes in verb form and word order.

Lesson 4

Whole class

Choose an official text which makes use of formal words and expressions, *e.g. notwithstanding, hereby, reside.* Prepare the text by covering up these words and expressions.
Read the text with the children, pausing for them to work out the concealed words. Reveal them to confirm, and write up as a list. Ask questions which probe the children's understanding of the text and especially of these words and expressions.
Ask children what they notice about the words in the list. Draw out the idea that they are formal; develop the idea by prompting children to suggest informal equivalents. Ask: Would words like this be appropriate in this context and for this purpose? Why not?
Work together to write other sentences including these formal words and expressions.

Group and independent work

Children read other official texts in the class collection, recording formal words and expressions, and less formal alternatives.

Differentiation

Low Attainers – Copymaster 32. Write less formal, more common alternatives for listed formal words.
High Attainers – Find, in the collection of texts, sentences which include formal words and expressions; rewrite them in less formal style.

Whole class

Ask children to contribute formal words and expressions they have found; add them to the list; explain what they mean; and suggest less formal equivalents.
Share sentences in which less formal words have been substituted; discuss the difference in tone and effect.

Lesson 5

Whole class

Together choose a school routine which includes several stages or processes, *e.g. playtimes or getting ready for PE.* Use a flow-chart to record aspects of it.
Explain that they are going to work together to write an official notice about this routine. Decide on what the first sentence should be about. Give children a few minutes to compose this, individually or in pairs. Share and discuss some sentences. Ask: Does it sound/read like a sentence from an official notice? Why? Why not? Prompt children to make changes to vocabulary and structure.
Use shared writing strategies to compose more of the text. Draw children's attention to the features of language and layout discussed in previous lessons, *e.g. what could they expand on in a footnote?*

As the work proceeds, give children opportunities to rework sentences, *e.g. into the passive.*

Group and independent work

Children write an official notice about a school routine of their own choice, using typical language and layout features, and working on large sheets of paper.

Differentiation

Low Attainers – Continue work begun in whole-class phase, or develop text from sentences written in Lesson 3.
High Attainers – Challenge children to use all the features, or to parody this kind of text by exaggerating them.

Whole class

Display sheets round the room; give children a few minutes to read them. Identify one feature of official texts; ask children who has used it, and share some examples. Repeat for other features.

Theme 7) Poetic devices and effects

Objectives

Text level:
- 3 to recognise how poets manipulate words (for quality of sound; connotations; layers of meaning)
- 5 to analyse how messages, moods, feelings and attitudes are conveyed in poetry
- 6 to read and interpret poems in which meanings are implied or multi-layered
- 14 to write commentaries

Sentence level:
- 3 to revise work on complex sentences

Word level:
- 2 to use known spellings as basis for spelling words with similar patterns

Resources
Single poet collections and anthologies of poetry providing a wide range of different styles; enlarged text versions of poems illustrating the devices highlighted in the theme (see below).
Copymasters 33 and 34, Homework 17

Assessment
At the end of this theme is the pupil able to:
- identify and discuss a range of different poetic styles and devices, and the effects they convey;
- contribute constructively to discussion of challenging poems, referring to the detail of the text to illustrate and justify points;
- write a detailed commentary on a poem, focusing on stylistic issues?

Lesson 1

Whole class

Explain that in this theme the children will be exploring the ways in which poets use words to create different effects.

Read aloud an extract from a poem with a striking rhythmic effect, *e.g. Auden's 'Night Mail', Noyes' 'The Highwayman'*. Ask children what they notice; focus their attention on rhythm. Identify and discuss the effect it creates and, where appropriate, the actions which it represents *e.g. steam train, galloping horse*.

Display an enlarged text version of the poem, and examine how the effect is created. Mark and clap out the pattern of beats in each line; identify line breaks, examine word choice.

Read the poem together, encouraging everyone to join in with a rhythmic reading. You could assign verses to different groups.

Read a poem with a contrasting rhythm. Identify the different effects and how these are created.

Group and independent work
Give each group a poem in which rhythm is an important element. Ask them to investigate how the rhythmic effect is conveyed, and to plan and rehearse a group reading aloud performance of the poem.

Differentiation
Low Attainers – Work with another extract from one of the poems read in whole class work.
High Attainers – Work with a poem in which the rhythm is more subtle and/or more varied.

Whole class
Ask a group to introduce and perform their poem. Ask others to comment on the rhythm and how it relates to the subject of the poem; and on how successfully the readers have conveyed the rhythm.
If time allows, repeat with another poem.

Lesson 2

Whole class

Ask children to imagine two scenes: one peaceful and quiet *e.g. sleeping baby, pond on a summer's day* and one full of movement and noise. Ask them to list verbs and adjectives to describe these scenes.

After a few minutes, pool words; write some up, choosing ones where the sound (as well as the meaning) matches the scene. Make this idea explicit, and relate it to word choice in poetry.

Read together an enlarged version of a poem in which words are used for the quality of their sound. Highlight and list these words. Experiment with substituting words with a similar meaning but different sound. How is the effect changed, weakened?

Look again at the collections of 'quiet' and 'noisy' words. Identify letters and letter strings that occur in each *e.g. quiet words with l, s, soft c, le, th, long vowel sounds*. Add similar words to the list. Revise work on spelling patterns.

Group and independent work
Give children copies of poems in which words are chosen for their sound; ask them to mark up and annotate the text to show this. Then record other words with the same sound qualities, underlining relevant letters and letter strings.

Differentiation
Low Attainers – Copymaster 33. Circle words chosen for quality of sound; write other quiet, peaceful words.
High Attainers – In addition, write a short commentary on use of sound in the poem.

Whole class
Ask children to share key 'sound words' in the poem they have been studying; ask others if they can work out the subject and the effect created.
List words beginning sn. Identify and discuss the (usually unpleasant) meanings associated with this sound.

Lesson 3

Whole class

Write up a word associated with a range of ideas, *e.g. gold, rose*. Ask children what things, ideas and feelings it makes them think about. Record and link these using a concept map. Explain that most words do not have just one single, simple meaning, but have associations that link them with a variety of meanings and contexts. Write up another word of this kind, and ask children to draw up a concept map for it. Share ideas to compile a class concept map.

Read together an enlarged text of a poem in which some words are chosen for their connotations. Identify one, and share ideas about what it brings to mind in the context of this poem. Identify another, and give children a couple of minutes to jot down associated ideas, then share them. Discuss how this use of words gives the poem a richer and more complex meaning.

Group and independent work

Give children a copy of a poem, and ask them to use highlighting and annotation to analyse and comment on the choice of words, drawing on work from the first three lessons (rhythm, sound, connotations).

Differentiation

Low Attainers – Circle words in the text for children to comment on.
High Attainers – Work with a poem with complex and challenging vocabulary.

Whole class

Ask children to share words they think have been chosen because of their associated meanings; to read the relevant part of the poem; and explain their ideas. Prompt others to share their ideas about the words.

Lesson 4

Whole class

In this lesson the focus is on figurative uses of language. Provide a stimulus for this way of thinking and using words by asking children to describe an object or creature *e.g. elephant, bat, fire extinguisher, pair of scissors* in terms of something else that it resembles in one way or another, *e.g. related to the five senses*.

As ideas are shared, remind children of previous work on similes and metaphors, and express ideas in both forms *e.g. its ears flapping like sails; its tree trunk legs*. Ask children to write one simile and one metaphor to describe the object or creature. Share these.

Read an enlarged text version of a poem which includes figurative language. Highlight and annotate relevant words and phrases; distinguish between similes and metaphors. Discuss their effect: How do they make us think and feel about the things being described? What do they contribute to the meaning and mood of the poem? Identify any recurring themes or patterns in the imagery used.

Group and independent work

Children browse anthologies to find examples of figurative language; choose ones that they feel are striking and effective; copy out the relevant lines for display.

Differentiation

Low Attainers – Select for children a poem in which simile and metaphor play a major part.
High Attainers – Copymaster 34. Annotate poem to show use of figurative language.

Whole class

Display lines including figurative language round the room, and give children a couple of minutes to read some. Share ideas about which are most powerful, puzzling, surprising ... Identify both the likeness being drawn and the use of language.

Lesson 5

Whole class

Display an enlarged text version of a challenging poem – one in which meanings are implicit and open to various interpretations. Read this aloud; then re-read it, asking children to follow the text. Give them a few minutes to jot down their first thoughts and impressions and any questions they have about the poem. Then share these with a partner. Prompt whole-class discussion with open-ended questions which lead children deeper into the poem, *e.g. What is the main idea/feeling? What is the poet trying to do? What is he/she really looking at? Inside him/herself? Outside him/herself? What is the movement of thought or feeling through the poem?*
As the discussion develops, encourage children to refer to the detail of the text to illustrate and support their ideas. Acknowledge that different views can be held. Explain that the children will be writing a commentary on this or another poem. Discuss how this might be organised, and draw on the discussion to write a few sentences together.

Group and independent work

Children plan and write a commentary on this poem, putting forward their own views, or on another challenging poem of their own choice. Ask them to refer to and quote from the text.

Differentiation

Low Attainers – Write extended answers to open questions about the poem discussed in whole-class work.
High Attainers – Encourage children to explore different possible interpretations and responses.

Whole class

Show the text of the poem again. Read a line or passage which has proved puzzling or open to debate. Ask children to share further thoughts on it. Repeat with other passages.

Theme 8) Poetic forms

Objectives

Text level:
- 3 to recognise how poets manipulate words
- 7 to identify key features of different types of literary text
- 9 to increase familiarity with significant poets of the past
- 10 to use different genres as models for writing

Sentence level:
- 3 to revise work on complex sentences

Word level:
- 7 to understand that the meanings of words change over time

Resources

Poetry anthologies including poems in a wide range of different forms (see below), and by poets both of past and present; enlarged text versions of some of these poems. An extract from the poem in free verse written out as prose.
Copymasters 35 and 36, Homework 18

Assessment

At the end of this theme is the pupil able to:
- identify defining features of different forms of poetry;
- discuss how poets manipulate words and sentences within these forms;
- identify and comment on language and other features of poems written in the past;
- write their own poems using different forms as models?

Lesson 1

Whole class

Explain that in this theme the children will be exploring different forms of poetry.
Read a poem with a striking and familiar form, *e.g. a limerick, a haiku, a conversation*. Ask the children to identify it, and explain how they can tell it is an example of this form. Repeat with one or two other forms.
Give pairs a few minutes to list all the poetic forms they know. Share, and compile a list.
Display an enlarged text version of a poem in a rhyming form. Identify and discuss its defining characteristics in more detail; draw attention as appropriate to rhyme scheme, organisation of lines in verses, rhythm, structure. Work together to write a definition of the form.
Identify and list the rhyming words in the poem. Give children a minute to list as many other rhymes for these words as they can. Share; identify various ways in which

the rhyme can be spelled. Look for opportunities to revise work on spelling of vowel phonemes.

Group and independent work

Assign a poetic form to each group; ask them to browse anthologies looking for examples of poems in this form; choose a representative example; and write a definition of the form.

Differentiation

Low Attainers – Book mark pages where examples of two or three forms are to be found
High Attainers – Challenge children to find unusual forms; write definitions.

Whole class

Ask one or two groups to introduce their poem, explaining what form it is in and what the characteristic features are; then read it aloud.
Discuss features that are essential to the form and ones that are optional.

Lesson 2

Whole class

Read an extract from a poem in free verse written in the past *e.g. from Wordsworth's 'Prelude', Matthew Arnold's 'Dover Beach' or a Shakespeare play*, displaying some or all of it as an enlarged text. Ask children what they notice; draw attention to the absence of rhyme. Ask pairs to discuss what makes it a poem and not prose. Share ideas. Examine how the language is patterned, *e.g. through rhythm and organisation in lines*.
Display the text of some of the poem written out as prose. Lead a whole-class reading of the two versions. Discuss how the effect differs, looking in particular at line-breaks and how they guide the reader.
Work through the extract, identifying sentence boundaries. Ask children what they notice about the structure and organisation of the sentences; whether these coincide with line breaks; whether the poet observes the usual conventions for punctuation.

Group and independent work

Give children the text of a poem in free verse written out as prose; ask them to read this, and to mark in where they think the line breaks come. Then give them a copy of the poem set out in the normal way. Compare their line-breaks with those of the poet.

Differentiation

Low Attainers – In addition, write a list of features which make the poem a poem.
High Attainers – In addition, write a reply to someone who says it isn't a poem.

Whole class

Pool and develop ideas about what makes the poem a poem.
Display prose and poem versions; examine effect of putting line breaks in different places.

Lesson 3

Whole class

In this lesson the focus is on rhyming forms. Prepare an enlarged text version of a sonnet or a poem in verses with a repeating pattern of rhyme in which most of the rhyming words are covered up. Read the poem together, pausing for children to work out the rhyming words, and revealing them to check.

Work out the pattern of rhyme. Explain and demonstrate how to record this using letters of the alphabet, e.g. *aabb for verses of Blake's 'The Tyger'*. Discuss the effect of rhyme in the poem, e.g. *to make it memorable and satisfying, to link words, to highlight rhythm*.

Give pairs of children a poetry anthology; ask them to find a poem that rhymes and to record the pattern in this way.

Review poems read so far in the theme that were written in the past. Identify words that are no longer commonly in use or that have a different meaning now.

Group and independent work

Children browse anthologies to find poems with as many different rhyme patterns as they can; record these patterns using alphabetical notation.

Differentiation

Low Attainers – Copymaster 35. Children match poems to notations of rhyme schemes.

High Attainers – Copymaster 36. Identify a less common rhyme scheme; complete pattern for following verses.

Whole class

Write up the letters for a rhyme scheme, e.g. *abab*. Ask children to contribute poems they have found with this pattern. Repeat for other rhyme schemes. Ask if they have found any others.

Lesson 4

Whole class

Write up a haiku; revise syllabic rules and other conventions of this form. If necessary, work through and reinforce counting of syllables, focusing on any words where this is tricky.

Show enlarged text versions of two tankas; ask children to read them in pairs, to deduce the rules (5:7:5:7;7), and write a definition of the form. Discuss how the content follows the pattern or lines. Introduce the term tanka.

Repeat this process for cinquains (2:4:6:8:2).

Discuss the general effect of very short forms like this, drawing attention to clarity and conciseness. What subjects are they most appropriate for?

Count the sentences in each of the poems read. Relate them to line-breaks. Identify and discuss points at which the poet modifies or breaks the usual conventions of sentence and punctuation, e.g. *changing usual word order, omitting words*.

Group and independent work

In groups or pairs, find and read other haiku, tankas and cinquains. Choose a favourite example of each form. Copy them out. Annotate the text, indicating whether it follows the rules exactly and other interesting features.

Differentiation

Low Attainers – Focus on one of these forms only.

High Attainers – Write a short commentary on one of their chosen poems, including analysis of sentence structure.

Whole class

Choose one of the forms; display examples round the room, and give children a few minutes to read them. Discuss which ones they would like to include in an anthology, and why. Prompt children to consider handling of the form as well as content and effect.

Lesson 5

Whole class

Choose one of the rhyming forms to use as a model. Recap features of the form. Decide together on a subject, and use a mind-map to generate and organise words that might be used in writing about it. Prompt children to think of rhyming pairs of words.

Use shared writing techniques to draft a verse in this form, focusing on rhyme.

Similarly, choose one of the syllabic forms, and an appropriate subject. Share words and ideas. Ask pairs of children to write one or two vivid, interesting sentences about the subject. Choose a sentence to work on together, and write it up. Give pairs a few minutes to rework and arrange the sentence so that it follows (or nearly follows) the rules of the form.

Write up some examples; work on them together to improve clarity and to match the conventions exactly.

Draw attention to issues of sentence structure and word choice.

Group and independent work

Children draft and revise their own poems modelled on a rhyming form and a syllabic form. Provide opportunities at other times for children to return to their poems and work on them in short bursts.

Differentiation

Low Attainers – Write a syllabic poem only; or adapt a poem read in a previous lesson.

High Attainers – Challenge children to follow all aspects of the rhyming form.

Whole class

Share work in progress. Identify and discuss the extent to which the children's poems follow the chosen form, and ways in which they might be improved.

Theme 9) Proverbs

Objectives

Text level:
- 7 to identify the key features of different kinds of literary texts
- 10 to use different genres as models for writing

Sentence level:
- 3 to revise work on complex sentences
- 4 to revise work on contracting sentences

Word level:
- 6 to collect and explain the meanings and origins of proverbs
- 7 to understand that the meanings of words change over time

Resources

Dictionaries and other collections of proverbs, e.g. The Oxford Dictionary of Proverbs, 'English Proverbs Explained' by Ridout and Witting; an enlarged text version of one page from this dictionary; other similar reference books, e.g. Brewer's Dictionary of Phrase and Fable.
Copymasters 37 and 38, Homework 19

Assessment

At the end of this theme is the pupil able to:
- recognise and comment on the function and characteristics of proverbs as a genre;
- identify the meaning and origins of specific proverbs;
- use knowledge of sentence types and structures to analyse proverbs;
- write concise proverbs, both original and modelled on existing examples;
- identify examples of change of word meaning over time?

Lesson 1

Whole class

Tell the class a proverb with a metaphorical basis, e.g. *Don't put all your eggs in one basket.* Ask them what this is called; introduce and define the term 'proverb'. Explain that in this theme they will be investigating the meanings, origins and language structures of proverbs. Write up five proverbs, and give children a few minutes to work out their meanings. Discuss these; draw out key features, e.g. *that proverbs express 'universal truths' or 'morals'; often use metaphors; are a traditional oral form.* Show and explain the function of a dictionary of proverbs. Display an enlarged text version of one page; identify and discuss how the material is organised (alphabetically or thematically), and what kind of information is provided. Give children copies of the dictionary or photocopied pages from it; work through the process of locating and reading entries.
Focus on a proverb which illustrates change in meaning over time (see Copymaster 37). Identify relevant words; compare meaning in the proverb with meaning now.

Group and independent work

Give children copies of, or photocopied extracts from, dictionaries of proverbs. Ask them to browse (within one letter or section), looking for proverbs that are interesting or puzzling. Set them challenges for finding proverbs about different subjects (*e.g. animals*) or 'morals' (*e.g. telling the truth*).

Differentiation

Low Attainers – Prepare a sheet with the first few words of common proverbs for children to look up and complete.
High Attainers – Copymaster 37. Identify (in proverbs) words that have a different meaning now; rewrite using contemporary equivalents.

Whole class

Ask children to contribute proverbs with particular features (e.g. metaphorical, puzzling); discuss meanings. Ask children who worked with Copymaster 37 to explain other examples of meaning change over time.

Lesson 2

Whole class

In the next two lessons the focus is on the grammatical structure of proverbs.
Explain that the wording of proverbs is intended to make them easy to remember. Write up examples that illustrate the following characteristic features:
- balanced constructions (*e.g. Two is company, three is a crowd*)
- use of internal rhyme and assonance (*e.g. There's many a slip 'twixt the cup and the lip*)
- imperatives (*e.g. Live and let live*)
- very short (*e.g. Much will have more, Murder will out*)
For each, ask children what they notice about structure and word choice. Draw out and discuss the general points. Divide the class into four groups, assigning a feature to each; give them a few minutes to find other proverbs which illustrate the feature. Share and discuss these.

Work out the meanings of proverbs which depend on metaphor or which are puzzling.

Group and independent work

Children search dictionaries or photocopied extracts for two proverbs to illustrate each of the four features.

Differentiation

Low Attainers – Give children a sheet with three examples of each feature; they match proverbs to features.
High Attainers – Challenge children to identify another language or structural feature of proverbs.

Whole class

Work through each feature in turn, asking children to suggest examples; write up some, and analyse their structure and wording. Ask others to work out their meanings.
Ask children to share ideas about other language features of proverbs, providing examples to illustrate.

Lesson 3

Whole class

Explain that in this lesson they will be looking at other grammatical features of proverbs.

Write up two proverbs: one which includes a main verb and one which does not (e.g. *More haste, less speed*). Ask: Which of these is not a sentence? Why? Identify and highlight the main verb. Give children a few minutes to find other examples; share some; identify main verbs in ones which are sentences.

Ask children what they notice about the tense of proverbs; draw out the idea that most are in the present; discuss why (making a statement about how things are). Look for examples of proverbs in other tenses (some are in the future). Look for opportunities to revise work on verb tense.

Explain that although most proverbs are short and simple in structure, some are longer and more complex.

Write up some examples (e.g. *People who live in glass houses should not throw stones, If at first you don't succeed, try, try and try again*). Analyse their structure and punctuation.

Group and independent work

Ask children to search for examples of proverbs with the kinds of grammatical features discussed in whole-class work.

Differentiation

Low Attainers – Copymaster 38. Distinguish between proverbs that are and are not sentences; find another example of each; circle main verbs in sentences

High Attainers – Focus on proverbs with more complex structures; write explanatory comments.

Whole class

Share proverbs illustrating each feature in turn. Write up interesting examples; mark up and annotate to show, *e.g. verb, tense, main clause, subordinate clause.*

Lesson 4

Whole class

Write up the first half of a literal proverb discussed previously in the unit, *e.g. He who hesitates . . .* Give the children a couple of minutes to compose a new ending, orally or in writing. Tell them they can have fun with this: their new proverbs do not need to be as earnest as the original. Share ideas; write up some. Repeat, writing up the beginning of a metaphorical proverb, *e.g. Don't count your chickens . . .*

Ask children if they can think of common first words for proverbs; compile a list (e.g. *Let, Better, Never, All*). Use shared writing techniques to compose proverbs starting with these words. You could prompt this by asking children to think of and discuss contemporary ideas around a theme such as money, or support it by writing new versions of an old proverb, perhaps using a different modern metaphor to express the idea.

During and after writing these new proverbs, draw children's attention back to the idea that proverbs should be short; prompt them to find ways of contracting the sentence and expressing the thought more concisely.

Group and independent work

Children write their new proverbs by changing the ending (or beginning) of existing proverbs, and/or by writing ones beginning with a common opening word.

Differentiation

Low Attainers – Using the sheet from Lesson 1, children write new endings for proverbs.

High Attainers – Encourage children to write new metaphorical proverbs.

Whole class

Ask children to share proverbs they have written; ask others to comment, drawing on their knowledge of characteristic stylistic and structural features. Is it clear and memorable? If it uses a metaphor, does this convey the general thought forcefully?

Lesson 5

Whole class

Start the lesson by asking pairs or small groups to agree on two proverbs that they have found especially interesting. Share and write up.

Choose one. Ask children to imagine the situations and stories that might lie behind these general statements of advice or right behaviour. Give children a few minutes to develop a simple story-line. They could record this in note form. Share ideas; choose one to develop together. Agree on a fictional genre (e.g. *fable, humorous, fantasy*) in which to tell the story. Briefly review the characteristic features of the genre, considering plot, character, setting and language.

Use shared writing techniques to compose the opening of the story; prompt children to use genre conventions, especially in relation to language.

Repeat, writing the story behind another proverb in another genre.

Group and independent work

Children choose a proverb that they find interesting, and write the story that might have given rise to it, working within the conventions of a chosen genre.

Differentiation

Low Attainers – Complete one of the stories begun in whole-class work.

High Attainers – Write a story which ends with one of the characters speaking the words of the proverb.

Whole class

Ask some children to share their stories. Ask the others to work out the proverb and the genre to which the story belongs, identifying conventions of language, plot and character which indicate this.

Theme 10 Argument and discussion

Objectives

Text level:
- 15 to recognise how arguments are constructed to be effective
- 16 to identify the features of balanced written arguments
- 18 to construct effective arguments
- 19 to write a balanced report of a controversial issue

Sentence level:
- 5 to investigate conditionals, construct sentences which express possibilities, hypotheses

Word level:
- 18 to build a bank of useful terms and phrases for argument

Resources
Texts which put forward an argument for or against a particular point of view; texts which present a balanced account of the various opinions held in relation to a particular issue. Choose examples which highlight use of conditional sentences and connectives in this context. Enlarged text versions of extracts from these texts. Factual and opinion pieces about a controversial issue. Copymasters 39 and 40, Homework 20

Assessment
At the end of this theme is the pupil able to:
- recognise and comment on the features of arguments and balanced reports of controversial issues;
- identify and compose conditional sentences;
- draw on a fund of connectives to use in articulating an argument of discussion;
- compose effective arguments and discussions, making use of the sentence and word level skills noted above?

Lesson 1

Whole class

Explain that in this theme the children will be looking at the language of argument and discussion.
Read with the children a text which argues strongly in favour of a particular point of view on an issue, presenting all or some of it in an enlarged version (the text should include examples of conditional sentences). Identify the writer's opinion and arguments put forward to support it, numbering these.
Focus on the language of the piece. Ask children to identify the structure of the argument, looking in particular at the sequencing and linking of points; at the use of examples and evidence to back up points.
Consider also whether other points of view are included, and if so, how *e.g. are they dismissed or answered?* Mark up and annotate the text.
Identify conditional sentences in the text and the part they play in the argument, *e.g. stating consequences and possibilities.* Discuss the structure of these sentences, and words which indicate conditionality, *e.g. if, then and modal auxiliary verbs such as might, will, would.*

Group and independent work
Children read similar texts, write a plan or outline of the writer's argument, and highlight language features discussed in whole-class work. Underline any conditional sentences, and circle key words.

Differentiation
Low Attainers – Copymaster 39. Fill gaps in conditional sentences; identify main points in the argument.
High Attainers – Write a commentary on the tactics used in the argument and their effectiveness.

Whole class
Share conditional sentences they have found; write up some, reviewing their structure and key words.
Ask children to read out points in arguments that they think are strongly and convincingly put; discuss why.

Lesson 2

Whole class

Read with the children a text which presents a balanced overview of the different opinions held on a controversial issue, presenting all or some of it in an enlarged version (the text should include examples of connecting words and phrases).
Ask children to identify similarities and differences between this and the text read in Lesson 1 (you could display this alongside). Draw out the idea that here the writer is not just arguing from and for one point of view, but considering a range of opinions. Identify these, and what the writer says about each, *e.g. identifying their strengths and weaknesses.* If the writer also states a personal view, identify where and how this is indicated. Mark up the text to show its structure.
Circle the first few words or phrases used to link ideas; prompt children to identify their function. Then ask them to find and list other examples in the text. Pool ideas together; discuss the exact function of each word or phrase.

Group and independent work
Children read similar texts, and analyse their structure, either by annotating them or by listing key points in sequence. Circle or list connecting words and phrases.

Differentiation
Low Attainers – Just highlight and list connecting words.
High Attainers – Deduce and record the plan the writer might have made before writing the piece.

Whole class
Pool connecting words found, and compile a list.
Ask children to explain the organisation of the text they have read. Demonstrate how to represent this visually, *e.g. as a diagram or flow-chart plus notes.*

Lesson 3

Whole class

Organise a short class debate on a controversial subject, *e.g. school uniforms, time spent watching TV, fox hunting.* When children have shared views for a few minutes, pause and review ideas from previous lessons, emphasising the structures and vocabulary of argument and features that help make an argument powerful, *e.g. evidence, examples, logical sequencing of ideas.* Give children a short 'time out' to choose one point to make, and to compose (orally or in writing) a sentence or two that expresses it clearly.

Share some of these ideas. Write up interesting examples, especially sentences which include conditionals or connectives; identify, highlight and discuss their structure.

Use shared writing strategies to extend this, *e.g. by*

composing sentences which illustrate language features the children are not using.

Group and independent work

Children write separate sentences that express various points of view about the issue that has been discussed. Display the list of connecting words for reference.

Differentiation

Low Attainers – Ask children to write two conditional sentences and two sentences using simpler connecting words.

High Attainers – Copymaster 40. Children write sentences linked by given connecting words and phrases.

Whole class

Ask children to contribute sentences which include a particular word, *e.g. might, if, would; therefore, so, similarly.* Write up and analyse some of these sentences; revise or edit as appropriate.

Lesson 4

Whole class

Agree with the children on a particular view to take on the issue discussed in the previous lesson (explain that they will have a chance to express their own later). Plan and make notes for an argument which expresses this view clearly and strongly: introduction; points in favour of the point of view, in sequence; evidence or examples to support each of these points. Decide whether to include other points of view, and, if so, how to deal with them, *e.g. by arguing against their logic or by providing evidence against them.*

Use shared writing strategies to write short paragraphs about one of the points and (if included) about another point of view.

Draw attention to the language features studied in previous lessons.

Group and independent work

Children apply skills and strategies from whole-class work to plan and write an argument expressing their own point of view on the subject

Differentiation

Low Attainers – Use a writing frame to focus and structure their argument.

High Attainers – Encourage children to refer to and counter opposing views.

Whole class

Ask children to read out one point from their argument. Ask the others to comment on its clarity and force: How could it be improved?

Ask children to share a paragraph in which they have identified and argued against another opinion. How have they countered it? Have they done so effectively?

Lesson 5

Whole class

Ask children who have expressed different views on the issue to summarise them. Write up an encapsulation of each.

Explain that they are now going to plan and start writing a balanced discussion of all these opinions. Choose a technique different from that used in the previous lesson and use it to plan the piece, *e.g. introduction; first point of view, considering its strengths and weaknesses, evidence for and against; second point of view ... etc.; conclusion.* Decide whether to come down in favour of one of these points of view, and if so at what point and how, *e.g. in the conclusion.*

Use shared writing strategies to write a paragraph about one of these points of view. Draw attention to the use of connectives, especially to indicate contrasts and

contradictions, *e.g. however, whereas, on the other hand, instead, nevertheless.*

Group and independent work

Children write their own balanced accounts of different views on this subject, following or adapting the plan outlined in whole class work. Display the list of relevant connectives for them to refer to.

Differentiation

Low Attainers – Prepare a writing frame for the children to use to structure their writing.

High Attainers – Ask children to include a statement of their own point of view.

Whole class

Bring the theme to a conclusion by holding a debate in which groups of children who share a particular view present it to the others, who respond with questions and counter arguments. Begin this now and continue outside this context.

Theme 1) Word play

Objectives

Word level:

- 2 to use known words as basis for spelling other words with similar patterns
- 3 to use independent spelling strategies
- 5 to invent words using known roots, prefixes and suffixes
- 6 to practise and extend vocabulary through word games
- 7 to experiment with language, creating new words

Resources

A collection of dictionaries.
Copymasters 41 and 42, Homework 21

Assessment

At the end of this theme is the pupil able to:
- invent new words, using knowledge of word derivation and other kinds of word formation;
- devise own words, games and puzzles;
- draw on word, sentence and text level knowledge to experiment and be inventive with language?

Lesson 1

Whole class

Explain that in this theme the children will be experimenting and playing with language in lots of different ways. In this first lesson the focus is on language play based on letters and the alphabet. Write up and explain an anagram of your name. Ask children to write anagrams of their first names on slips of paper, if possible making another word, e.g. Karl into lark. Share round for others to solve. Work in pairs to find words that can be made into other words by rearranging all the letters, e.g. once/cone, words/sword. Share.
Explain examples of language play based on constraints on the use of certain letters:
- lipograms: one vowel banned;
- univocalics: all but one of the vowels banned;
- pangrams: sentence in which every letter of the alphabet is used once only. 'The quick brown fox jumps over the lazy dog' is a an attempt at this.
- sentences in which words begin with consecutive letters

of the alphabet, e.g. 'All boys can drive . . .' but not necessarily starting from A.
Use shared writing techniques to compose such texts, e.g. the opening of a well known traditional tale.

Group and independent work

Set anagram puzzles for others to solve. Experiment with writing texts or sentences following the various constraints on letter use.

Differentiation

Low Attainers – Rewrite the beginning of another traditional tale without using o.
High Attainers – Try pangrams and sentences with initial letters in alphabetical order.

Whole class

Share and write up word-for-word anagrams; ask class to solve them.
Share texts written with letter constraints; identify and discuss problems, e.g. how to avoid common words that include banned letters.

Lesson 2

Whole class

Write up a simple sentence, e.g. The woman opened the door. Work together to 'stretch' it by adding clauses and phrases. Give children a few minutes to experiment with this. Share sentences.
Ask children to write a sentence following a basic structure on a strip of paper in large letters (see Copymaster 41 for a simple example); and then cut it up into parts. Make a pile for each part, and share them out so that each child gets one from each. Make the (probably silly) sentence that results; share these.
Organise the class to compose a three-sentence story: each child writes a beginning sentence on a piece of paper with their name on it; passes it on for someone to write the 'middle', and then again for someone to write the end. Return texts to the first children; read the stories aloud; give them titles.

Explain text messages on mobile phones; because there is very little space, various kinds of abbreviation are used. Write up some, e.g. CU; Gr8; 2day. (See Homework 21 for others.) Ask children to work them out. Invent others together.

Group and independent work

Write the longest sensible 'stretched' sentence they can. Write their own three sentence story. Write a phone text message using abbreviated forms.

Differentiation

Low Attainers – Copymaster 41. Compose sentences with a given structure; cut out parts; make new sentences.
High Attainers – Write an interesting, exciting story consisting a maximum of 50 words.

Whole class

Share work from independent work. Which are the best, funniest stretched sentences, three-sentence stories and phone text messages? Why?

Lesson 3

Whole class

In this lesson the focus is on inventing new words. Write up an assortment of Greek and Latin word parts. Ask children to identify what they mean and to suggest words in which they occur. Talk through the process of inventing new words by combining these word parts in new ways, *e.g. if phono means 'sound' and phobia means 'fear of' then phonophobia means . . .* Give children, working in pairs, a few minutes to invent new words drawing on work on word roots from Term 1. Share these, asking others to work out what they mean.

Similarly, invent new words ending in suffixes which carry a specific meaning, *e.g. flatlet, biggish, homewards.* Write up examples of words formed by contraction, *e.g. zoo, exam, fridge;* by blending two words, *e.g. smog from smoke and fog, camcorder from camera and recorder;* and by forming a pronounceable word from initial letters of a phrase (acronyms), *e.g. scuba from self-contained underwater breathing apparatus.* Work together to invent new words in these ways, *e.g. lufa – line up for assembly.*

Group and independent work

Invent new words from known roots, prefixes and suffixes; by contraction and blending, and by inventing acronyms. Write dictionary entries for these words, defining their meaning, explaining their derivation, and using them in illustrative sentences.

Differentiation

Low Attainers – Write full and contracted versions of words, *e.g. pop, popular.*
High Attainers – Write sets of new words, related by structure (*e.g. all with same root*) or by meaning (*e.g. all to do with school dinners*).

Whole class

Share invented words; ask others to work out their meaning and derivation.
Plan how to collect these words in a class Dictionary of New Words.

Lesson 4

Whole class

Write up the words 'saucepan thermometer'; ask the children what animal they can find hidden here (panther). Give them a few minutes to experiment with hiding other animal words between two words. Choose children to write up their words; ask others to find the animal.

Tell the children two or three jokes which depend on puns. Explain that they exploit the sound similarity between words (*e.g. court and caught*) or the fact that some words (*e.g. nut, bar, draw*) have more than one meaning. Share other jokes of this type. Brainstorm and list words that have more than one meaning; give children time out to create a joke based on them. Tell the jokes.
Write up the word pairs have/save, mother/bother, early/dearly, clown/blown. Ask children what they notice: the words look the same but sound different. Explain that pairs of words like this are called eye-rhymes. Give children time to write other such pairs or sets. Share.
Work together to write a rhyming couplet using eye-rhymes.

Group and independent work

Children hide another category of words, *e.g. colours, food,* between two words. Using a dictionary will help them to find the second of these words.
Search joke books for jokes using puns and sound similarity, *e.g. Knock-knock jokes. Invent their own jokes.*

Differentiation

Low Attainers – Copymaster 42. Complete pairs of eye rhymes.
High Attainers – Write a poem using eye-rhymes on a large sheet of paper.

Whole class

Ask children to display and read their eye-rhyme poems. Discuss effect.
Share jokes – and kill them by analysing how they work!

Lesson 5

Whole class

In this lesson the focus is on word games. Explain and demonstrate the following word games; involve children in both solving and setting them:
• Sharon's game: like Hangman but letters have to be guessed in order; relate to work on possible and impossible letter sequences;
• building chains of words (usually in the same category) in which words begin with the final letter of the preceding word, *e.g. ostrich – hawk – kestrel – lark;*
• give a sequence of three letters in alphabetical order, *e.g. LMN; find a word in which they occur in this order: lemon.*
• word columns in which one word is transformed into another changing only one letter at a time, and making a word at each step, *e.g. dog: dot: cot: cat.*

Group and independent work

Organise children to play these games in groups and, in the case of the last two, to set puzzles for others to solve.

Differentiation

Low Attainers – Written chains of words linked by final/initial letters; set as a puzzle by deleting some of the words for others to work out.
High Attainers – Focus on the challenging task of setting word column puzzles.

Whole class

Play Word 20 Questions: someone thinks of a word; others try to work out what it is by asking questions which do not relate to its meaning.

Theme 2) Advertisements: a language investigation

Objectives

Text level:
- 19 to review a range of non-fiction text types and their characteristics
- 22 to select the appropriate style and form to suit a specific purpose and audience

Sentence level:
- 1 to revise the language conventions and grammatical features of different types of text (persuasive)
- 2 to conduct detailed language investigations

Word level:
- 6 to practise and extend vocabulary
- 7 to experiment with language

Resources
A collection of print advertisements illustrating the language features indicated in lesson plans; enlarged versions of these, *e.g. photocopies or text copied out; appropriate magazines and newspapers for children to search for such advertisements.*
Copymasters 43 and 44, Homework 22

Assessment
At the end of this theme is the pupil able to:
- identify and discuss the language features of advertisements;
- critically evaluate an advertisement, considering intended effects and strategies used;
- experiment with language to write their own advertisement, matching text to intended audience and effect?

Lesson 1

Whole class

Prepare for this lesson by writing up prompts for discussion of text-level features of advertisements, *e.g. selling point? appeal? persuasive techniques? figurative language? rhythm, rhyme and alliteration?*
Explain that in this theme they will be investigating the language of advertisement in detail, and writing their own advertisements.
Give pairs of children a couple of minutes to share favourite or memorable advertisements – from television as well as print. Share some as a class; prompt children to explain what they liked about them and how they worked. Display an advertisement. Give pairs time out to discuss it, focusing on prompts.
Choose a prompt, and ask a pair to report what they noticed; ask others to develop and add to these comments. Repeat for other prompts. Link with previous work on features of persuasive texts.

Group and independent work
Children search the collection of advertisements or magazines and newspapers for advertisements. Choose one; examine it in relation to the issues discussed in whole-class work. Record their ideas by writing the first paragraph of an explanatory caption which they will add to in Lessons 2 and 3.

Differentiation
Low Attainers – Copymaster 43. Read and write about an advertisement with clear and striking language features.
High Attainers – Write a comparison of two advertisements for the same kind of product.

Whole class
Monitor work to identify advertisements that are especially interesting in terms of issues in this lesson; ask children who have worked on these to share their ideas. Ask others to identify similarities and differences with own advertisements.

Lesson 2

Whole class

Prepare for this lesson by writing up prompts for discussion of sentence-level features of advertisements, *e.g. short? verbless? unusual, eye-catching structures? questions? tag phrases and jingles?*
Give pairs of children time out to study an advertisement with a good deal of text. After a few minutes, ask them to share interesting and unusual sentences, commenting on them in relation to the prompt questions.
Write up and analyse examples, prompting children to draw on previous work on sentence structure and punctuation. Focus in particular on ways in which 'rules' are bent or broken (*e.g. beginning with a conjunction*) and the reasons for this. (It makes the reader take notice.)
Ask children to identify any tag phrases (*e.g. Put a tiger in your tank, Probably the best . . .*); discuss what makes them memorable. Share other tag phrases and jingles, including ones used in TV advertisements.

Group and independent work
Read other advertisements. Find and record unusual or striking sentence structures, using prompts as headings. Write out any tag phrases on strips of paper.

Differentiation
Low Attainers – Re-read Copymaster 43 from Lesson 1; identify and copy out sentences with interesting and unusual features.
High Attainers – Write a detailed commentary on typical sentence-level features of advertisements, giving examples.

Whole class
Choose one of the prompts. Share and discuss examples found, identifying unusual features.
Share and write up tag phrases; discuss which is the most effective and why. Plan how to organise a display of the tag phrases collected, considering how they might be categorised.

Lesson 3

Whole class

Display around the room a collection of advertisements with interesting and unusual word-level features (see below). Give children a few minutes to study them, to make notes and to copy out words that catch their attention. Share ideas. As the discussion develops, identify and discuss examples of the following typical features:
• use of comparatives and superlatives, *e.g. More for your money. Fastest ever.* Discuss whether the basis of the comparison is clear.
• vivid, concrete words, especially adjectives, *e.g. dew-fresh*
• word play, including invented names for products, puns (*e.g. Go to work on an egg*)
• deviant spellings, *e.g. cuppa, kwik, nite.* Identify the spelling pattern that has been 'broken'
Write up lists of words under these headings. Discuss the effects they create and why advertisers use words in these ways.

Ask children to jot down some words commonly used in advertisement, *e.g. new, best, only, ultimate, ideal, unmatched, finest, tested, improved.* Pool ideas and draw up a list. Discuss reasons, developing discussion of selling points and persuasive techniques from lesson.

Group and independent work

Examine other advertisements. Find examples of characteristic word level features, and record them in an organised way on a large sheet of paper.

Differentiation

Low Attainers – Find examples of just one feature, *e.g. vivid adjectives, comparatives and superlatives.*
High Attainers – Copymaster 44. Write about word choice in an advertisement; rewrite to create a different effect.

Whole class

Share and discuss examples of word use of the types identified in whole-class work.
Read out and discuss advertisement on the Copymaster; share new versions.

Lesson 4

Whole class

Explain that in the next two lessons they will be planning, writing and evaluating a newspaper advertising campaign for a new kind of chocolate bar or ice-cream. Quickly share information about existing kinds of chocolate bars and ice-creams, and possibilities for new ones. Decide on one.
Discuss and make decisions about the selling point and appeal of this new product. What shall we say about it? How can we get people interested in it?
Brainstorm and record possible names, including invented words and deviant spellings. Discuss associations and effect of each; choose one.
Use shared writing techniques to compose tag phrases and sentences about the product, drawing on work from previous lessons.

Group and independent work

Organise children to work on groups to decide on a product and a name; to draft a magazine or newspaper advertisement for it. Work on this will need to continue in other literacy hours with input on relevant language issues, and outside this context.

Differentiation

Low Attainers – Write an advertisement with just one tag phrase and one sentence.
High Attainers – Draft at least two different advertisements and assess reactions to them.

Whole class

As work proceeds, draw children together to discuss techniques they can use to evaluate their advertisements.

Lesson 5

Whole class

Monitor the groups' work to choose advertisements that raise a range of interesting language issues.
Display one, and ask the group to explain the thinking behind their choice of product name and the advertising 'copy'.
Prompt other children to comment. As the discussion develops, focus in on the text, sentence and word level issues and features highlighted in Lessons 1–3 and consider possibilities for changing and improving the advertisement. Repeat with another advertisement.
Focus in turn on each of the characteristic language features of advertisements identified in the theme, and ask children to share examples of how they have used them in their own advertisements. Identify and revisit features that are being ignored or poorly used; discuss ways in which they can be used more effectively.

Group and independent work

Children revise and improve their advertisements, taking into account feedback from research and making more and more effective use of language features. Produce a full-page newspaper or magazine advertisement.

Differentiation

Low Attainers – Suggest focuses for rewriting, *e.g. add an adjective; shorten.*
High Attainers – Encourage children to write an advertisement with a substantial amount of 'copy'.

Whole class

Ask groups to present work in progress, explaining the changes they are making and why. Prompt children to identify and discuss uses of characteristic features. Work together to plan and organise a display of the finished advertisements, including early drafts, completed questionnaires, interview notes, etc.

Theme 3) Comparing novelists and novels

Objectives

Text level:
- 1 to describe and evaluate the style of an individual writer
- 5 to compare and contrast the work of a single writer
- 6 to look at connections and contrasts in the work of different writers
- 8 to use a reading journal effectively
- 12 to compare texts in writing

Sentence level:
- 1 to revise the language conventions and grammar of different types of text (narrative)
- 4 to secure control of complex sentences

Resources

Copies of several novels by the same author, if possible one with whom they have some familiarity but whose work they have not studied in detail; novels by other authors whose work contrasts in theme and style;

enlarged text versions of representative extracts from these novels. NOTE Work on this unit should be accompanied by opportunities for independent reading of the work of these novelists and by reading of a book by the featured novelist as the class novel.
Copymasters 45 and 46, Homework 23

Assessment

At the end of this theme is the pupil able to:
- identify and discuss the characteristic features of the work of a novelist;
- note range and variation within the work of this novelist;
- compare the work of this novelist with that of another, noting similarities and differences in thematic concerns and style;
- use a reading journal to note and develop their responses to a novel;
- plan and write a comparison of the work of two novelists;
- identify and comment on the characteristic language features of narrative writing?

Lesson 1

Whole class

Explain that they will be exploring the work of one novelist and comparing it with that of other novelists. Introduce the featured novelist; prompt children to share what they know about this author and his/her work. Read a representative extract from one of his/her novels, presenting some of it as an enlarged text. Write up a list of aspects of fiction to focus children's attention, *e.g. theme, language, setting, characters, mood, genre.* Give them a few minutes to re-read the enlarged text, and jot down ideas under these headings.
Share ideas and personal responses. As the discussion proceeds, jot up a selection of the children's ideas and responses.
Explain that what they have been doing together is keeping a joint reading journal. Introduce and explain this term, or extend children's understanding of it.
Return to the enlarged text; ask children to re-read a

prose passage (not dialogue), and to comment on the author's style, focusing on sentence structure.

Group and independent work

Organise groups to read the same extract from this or another novel by the author together, pausing frequently to discuss their responses to the text. Give one children the role of scribe who notes down the group's thoughts, using Copymaster 45.

Differentiation

Low Attainers – Mark in stopping points, with prompts for discussion: *Pause here to talk about . . .*
High Attainers – Encourage children to focus on aspects of language and structure.

Whole class

Ask scribes to share notes they have made of their group's responses to the text. Compare approaches, considering both what groups have discussed and how it has been recorded. Draw out points to develop understanding of how to use a reading journal.

Lesson 2

Whole class

Read with the class an extract from another novel by the featured author, presenting some or all of it as an enlarged text. Ask children how they can tell it is by the same author. Give them a few minutes to note down similarities. Share ideas, compiling a list of similarities. Ask them now if they can see any differences between the two extracts. Divide the class into groups, giving each an aspect of fiction to focus on (see Lesson 1). Share and record, compiling a second list. Draw out the general idea that an author's work has defining characteristics, but that within this there is also usually variation. Ask children to take on the role of fiction editor whose task is to write a catalogue entry introducing this novelist's work. Work together to write a few sentences for the catalogue.

Group and independent work

Children read other extracts from novels by the featured author, and use a reading journal to note their responses and further similarities and differences. Write a short description of the author's work, as if for a publisher's catalogue.

Differentiation

Low Attainers – Design and write a poster advertising the author's work.
High Attainers – Write a more extended comment on the author's work, including critical evaluation.

Whole class

Introduce for discussion aspects of response to the author's work which have been highlighted previously. Ask children to scan their reading journal notes for references to these issues, and to draw on them to join in the discussion.

Lesson 3

Whole class

Read with the children an extract from a novel by another author, presenting some of it as an enlarged text. Ask them how they can tell it is written by someone else. Share first thoughts. Organise groups as before, but this time ask them to consider all aspects of fiction and to identify as many differences between the two authors as they can. After a few minutes, pool ideas to compile a two-column list of differences (Author 1/Author 2), organised under headings, e.g. theme, characters, style. Highlight and annotate the enlarged text to show these features.

Ask children whether they can see any similarities between the work of the two authors. Clarify these by composing sentences beginning 'Both novelists ...' Re-read the enlarged text extracts from the two authors, focusing on prose passages rather than dialogue. Ask children to identify any differences in style at sentence-level (e.g. preference for short/long, simple/complex sentences, use of punctuation).

Group and independent work

Children read extracts from the work of another novelist; use a reading journal to record their responses and what they notice about content and style. Draw on this and the notes they made in the previous lesson to compile their own lists of similarities and differences in the work of this and the featured novelist.

Differentiation

Low Attainers – Copymaster 46. Read and note differences between two strikingly contrasting extracts.
High Attainers – Ask children to focus on aspects of style and language.

Whole class

Ask children to present their comparison of two novelists, illustrating this with quotations. Look for opportunities to develop understanding of aspects of fiction and the characteristics of the featured novelist.

Lesson 4

Whole class

Re-read one of the extracts from Lessons 1–3. Remind children of work they have done in previous years about different kinds of texts, and ask them how they can tell that this is from a narrative. Give them a few minutes to jot down ideas, then share. Identify and develop through discussion the following features:
* use of past tense (except in dialogue): find and underline verbs;
* imagined, specific subject matter;
* chronological organisation of events. Identify sequence, and any departures from chronological ordering, e.g. in brief flashbacks;
* use of temporal connectives to indicate chronological sequence. Find and circle these, noting the function of each;
* use of descriptive language to realise specific events, characters, settings;
* use of dialogue.

Where appropriate, make comparisons with the features of other text types, especially non-chronological reports.

Group and independent work

Re-read one of the extracts they have worked with in an earlier lesson; identify examples of the use of these features, by marking up and annotation, or by making notes. Note any cases where they do not apply (e.g. novel in present tense, extract without dialogue). Display list of features for children to refer to.

Differentiation

Low Attainers – Highlight examples of relevant features in the text for children to identify and name.
High Attainers – Write a commentary on the author's use and handling of these conventions.

Whole class

Work through each feature in turn, asking children to contribute an example of its use and any texts in which it was not present. Identify any other features which all the texts shared.

Lesson 5

Whole class

Return to the notes made about the featured novelist and the novelist discussed in Lesson 3. Recap and extend discussion of similarities and differences, prompting children to incorporate ideas from Lesson 4.
Use shared writing techniques to plan a non-chronological report in which their work is compared. Discuss and evaluate different ways of organising this, e.g. by novelist or by aspects of fiction, e.g. Style, Themes, etc. Which way would make the comparison clearest? Work together to draft a section of the comparison. Give children a few minutes to note ideas and examples. Ask them to suggest an opening sentence. Write up possibilities; confirm that they are in the appropriate style; look for opportunities to revise features of this non-fiction text type.

Group and independent work

Drawing on notes from previous lessons, children plan and begin writing their own comparison of two novelists.

Differentiation

Low Attainers – Offer children a writing frame or structure of sub-headings.
High Attainers – Prompt children to include introduction and conclusion, and to make evaluative comments. This activity provides a context for more extended writing.

Whole class

Share work in progress. Discuss in terms of content and of the organisation and style appropriate to this kind of text.

Theme 4) Explanatory texts

Objectives

Text level:
- 15 to secure understanding of the features of explanatory texts
- 16 to identify the key features of impersonal formal language
- 20 to secure control of impersonal writing
- 21 to divide whole texts into paragraphs

Sentence level:
- 1 to revise the language conventions and grammatical features of different types of text (explanatory)
- 3 to revise formal styles of writing

Word level:
- 1 to identify mis-spellings

Resources
A range of explanatory texts, linked where possible to work in other areas of the curriculum, e.g. explanations of processes and systems in biology, geography, manufacturing; of how to carry out procedures in maths or science. Large text extracts from some of these.
Copymasters 47 and 48, Homework 24

Assessment
At the end of this theme is the pupil able to:
- identify and comment on the features of explanatory writing at text, sentence and word levels;
- write an explanatory text of their own including these features;
- organise their writing in well-focused paragraphs, coherently linked;
- write sentences in a formal, impersonal style; revise them to improve clarity?

Lesson 1

Whole class

Organise the class into groups, and give each a different explanatory text. Ask children to read it together, and then to identify and discuss its purpose and features. After a few minutes, ask each group to share their ideas about the text with the class. As the discussion develops, prompt children to focus on what the texts have in common. Identify the purpose that all the texts serve (to explain the how and why of something) and their text-level features, e.g. sequencing of information, often in chronological order; introductions and conclusions; use of diagrams, flow-charts, etc. to represent processes graphically. List these on the board.
Prompt children to discuss what matters most in this kind of writing; emphasise importance of organisation, clarity and coherence. Ask children to re-read their text, evaluating their success in relation to these criteria. Share ideas.

Group and independent work
Children scan non-fiction looking for other examples of explanatory texts. Read them; note subject matter and text-level features; write a short evaluation focused on the criteria identified in whole-class work.

Differentiation
Low Attainers – Children work with a text which displays features clearly.
High Attainers – Children work with sophisticated, challenging examples of this text type.

Whole class
Display list of purposes and features of explanatory writing. Ask children to comment on each in turn in relation to the text they have been reading. Develop understanding of the genre and variations within it.

Lesson 2

Whole class

Display and read with the children an enlarged text version of a piece of explanatory writing. Give children (working individually or in pairs) a few minutes to re-read it and make notes about vocabulary and sentence structure. Pool ideas about vocabulary. Focus on:
- technical or specialist terms and whether these are explained;
- connectives. Highlight these, and identify their function: typically to indicate temporal or causal relationships. If there are several, ask children to classify them, and add others to each set.

Underline sentences typical of the text types, e.g. complex structures reflecting complex relationships; passive verbs; conditional sentences indicating alternatives and hypothetical situations. Ask children to read these carefully, and comment on them. If necessary prompt this by asking: Can you find a sentence that ...? Revise or extend understanding of these structures, as appropriate.

Group and independent work
Children re-read the explanatory texts they used in Lesson 1, looking for word and sentence features identified in whole-class work. Highlight and annotate the text, or record features under headings, e.g. connectives indicating time, passive verbs, conditional sentences.

Differentiation
Low Attainers – Copymaster 47. Annotate a text to show word and sentence level features of explanatory writing.
High Attainers – In addition, write a short commentary on vocabulary and sentence structure.

Whole class
Ask children to share examples of sentence-level features. Write up, confirm and examine some. Pool connectives found; compile or extend lists for temporal or logical functions.

Lesson 3
Whole class

Recap the discussion in Lesson 1 of topics which offer appropriate material for explanatory writing. Identify similar possibilities in recent work in other curriculum areas, focusing attention on processes, systems and procedures. Agree on one to write about together. Share ideas about this topic, prompting children to explain hows and whys (not just to describe 'what happens'). Jot down key words and ideas.

Remind children of the importance of sequencing this material in a clear temporal and/or logical order. Identify what comes first, and next ... Discuss and decide on a planning technique which would suit this kind of writing, *e.g. flow charts*.

Give individuals or pairs a few minutes to use this technique to plan the first few 'steps' of the piece. Share contributions; develop and record a joint plan. Discuss whether introduction and/or conclusion are needed, and how diagrams could be used. Indicate these on the plan. Explain how this plan can form the basis for structuring the written text in paragraphs.

Group and independent work
Children plan a piece of explanatory writing on a topic of their own choice related to curriculum or outside school interests, using a flow chart (Copymaster 48 is provided for this) or another appropriate technique.

Differentiation
Low Attainers – Complete a plan for the topic discussed in whole-class work.
High Attainers – Annotate their plan with key words, notes, etc.

Whole class
Share and talk through some topics and plans, focusing on what is being explained. Emphasise again how this plan can be used to focus and organise the text in paragraphs.

Lesson 4
Whole class

Return to the plan. Give children a few minutes to draft opening sentences for the introduction and the first section proper. Share and write up contributions. Check that language conventions and grammatical features are appropriate, focusing in particular on impersonal style (not in first person); the use (in most cases) of the simple present tense and passive verbs (e.g. The cocoa pods are laid out to dry); connecting words and phrases. Highlight and annotate the sentences to show these features.

Use shared writing strategies to compose the first two or three paragraphs. Explain how the information in each paragraph is centred round one key idea. When moving from one paragraph to the next, explain how they can be linked (*e.g., by pronoun and connecting words*) to make a coherent text. Mark up these links.

Where appropriate, decide where diagrams could be used and what accompanying text (*e.g. labels, caption*) is needed.

Group and independent work
Children draft the explanatory texts they planned. This provides a context for extended writing which children can return to in subsequent literacy hours and/or at other times. Display the list of connectives for reference.

Differentiation
Low Attainers – Write just one or two sentences for each 'step' of the process they are explaining.
High Attainers – Read the first few paragraphs; point out conventions and features they could be using.

Whole class
Share work in progress. Identify conventions that are being used, and ones that could be introduced or used more fully.
Look at the role played by diagrams.

Lesson 5
Whole class

Revise strategies for identifying mis-spellings, *e.g. does not look right, breaks a rule, known difficult word*.
Ask children to read their drafts, to circle words they think are mis-spelt, and to underline the relevant part of the word. Ask those using computers to make a note of words the spell-checker identifies as errors. Share and write up some contributions; confirm whether they are errors; identify (where possible) their causes; correct them. Remind children about the kind of errors that are not picked up by a spell-checker, e.g. *proper names, errors that are the correct spelling of another word*. With their author's permission, share extracts from selected drafts. Ask children to identify strengths and points for improvement. Discuss these in relation to the general criteria for this kind of text, their specific language conventions and grammatical features, and the organisation and linking of paragraphs.
Use shared writing techniques to revise and edit.

Group and independent work
Children read their drafts; annotate them to indicate areas for improvement; revise and edit. This work is also likely to extend beyond a single literacy hour.

Differentiation
Low Attainers – 'Mark' some of the draft for them, indicating a small number of things that might be changed or added.
High Attainers – Encourage children to focus on language conventions, and improving clarity.

Whole class
Display some drafts and revisions around the room, and give children time to read them. Choose some to compare and evaluate as a class, identifying what has been changed and why.

Theme 5) Extended story writing

Objectives

Text level:
- 14 to write an extended story on a theme identified in reading
- 7 to annotate passages in response to specific questions

Sentence level:
- 1 to revise language conventions and grammatical features of different types of text (narrative)
- 4 to secure control of complex sentences

Word level:
- 1 to identify mis-spelt words
- 3 to use independent spelling strategies
- 6 to practise and extend vocabulary
- 7 to experiment with language (similes and metaphors)

Resources
Enlarged text extracts from a story with which the children are familiar.
NOTE Children will need time after Lesson 4 to draft their stories independently.
Copymasters 49 and 50, Homework 25

Assessment
At the end of this theme is the pupil able to:
- plan and draft an extended story;
- experiment with word choice and figurative language in narrative writing;
- use conventions of narrative writing confidently for their own purposes;
- annotate and revise a draft to produce an improved and polished final version;
- identify words they are not sure how to spell, and develop strategies for attempting and checking them?

Lesson 1

Whole class

Explain that in this theme the children will be planning, drafting and revising their own story.
Read an extract from a familiar novel, presenting some of it as an enlarged text. Ask: What possibilities for writing other stories does this suggest? Encourage children to share ideas; focus and develop this by prompting them to consider different elements (setting, character, plot, genre) and different strategies (continuation, changing an element, adding a new element). Record ideas on the board. Remind children of links between stories they have identified in their reading, *e.g. modern versions of fairy stories, sequels and series, stories with similar settings or themes.*
Generalise to other stories, and set the task for the unit: that they will be planning a story related in one way or another to a story that they know.

Ask children what they notice about the style of the novel, *e.g. use of dialogue, word choice, figurative language, genre features.* Discuss how this might suggest possibilities for their own story.

Group and independent work
Children review novels and short stories they have read, decide on one to use as the basis for their own story, and write a 'brief' for it.

Differentiation
Low Attainers – Work out an idea for developing the story discussed in whole-class work.
High Attainers – Encourage children to consider style and genre as well as content.

Whole class
Ask children to share ideas for their stories, explaining how they are going to use the source novel.

Lesson 2

Whole class

Choose an idea for a new story based on the one explored in Lesson 1. Discuss and develop this idea with children; make some quick decisions together about the setting and characters involved, and on the first few episodes in the plot. Record these on the board.
Talk through and demonstrate various ways of planning a story more systematically, drawing out the different emphasis and potential of each. *You could use:*
- a story ladder or time-line to chart the sequence of events; explain how this could be annotated to show other aspects, *e.g. setting.*
- a chart organised in terms of different story elements: plot, characters, setting.
- a chart organised in terms of underlying narrative structure, *e.g. Opening situation, Problem, Developing conflict, Climax, Resolution.*
Work together to write an opening sentence for the

story, experimenting with alternatives. Revise the language conventions of narrative writing.

Group and independent work
Children use one of the planning techniques to develop their story idea, working on large sheets of paper. Explain that the storyline should involve a relatively small number of events (to ensure that there is time to develop elements other than plot).

Differentiation
Low Attainers – Copymaster 49. Chart for planning under headings related to story elements.
High Attainers – Copymaster 50. Chart for planning underlying narrative structure.

Whole class
Monitor group work to choose interesting examples of each technique. Display these; identify and discuss issues raised by working in these ways and how the technique could be used more effectively.

Lesson 3

Whole class

Choose from the story used in Lesson 1 an extract where the focus is on characterisation and includes some dialogue. Read this to the children, presenting some or all of it as an enlarged text.

Prompt them to identify and discuss what they learn about the characters.

Switch the focus to how this information is conveyed. Draw their attention, as appropriate, to direct description of character and relationships; interior monologue; characterisation through dialogue and action.

Choose one character from the story being developed with the class. Give pairs of children a few minutes to discuss what he/she is like and his/her relationships with other characters in the story. Then ask them to compose a sentence describing them; a short dialogue exchange with another character; and a thought or feeling, e.g. beginning 'X knew that ... felt that....'

Share contributions, discussing how each strategy can be used to develop the characters in their stories.

Group and independent work

Children write brief sketches of the main characters in the story they are developing, using the three techniques introduced in whole-class work.

Differentiation

Low Attainers – Draw a quick sketch of each character; add a thought bubble and a speech bubble.

High Attainers – Encourage children to focus on ways of conveying thoughts and feelings.

Whole class

Ask two or three children to share their character sketches. Discuss ways of introducing and describing a character's thoughts and feelings, recording wordings.

Lesson 4

Whole class

Choose from the story used in Lesson 1 an extract where the focus is on description of setting and atmosphere. Read this to the children, presenting some or all of it as an enlarged text.

Identify and discuss how the setting for the story is described and the atmosphere evoked. Draw their attention to word choice and to any uses of figurative language.

Identify the setting for the story they are developing as a class; use a mind map to generate words and phrases to describe it. Encourage children to search their vocabularies for vivid and accurate words.

Prompt children to think about what various aspects of the setting remind them of or are like; use this to create similes and metaphors to describe it. Write them up.

Give children (individually or in pairs) a few minutes to draw on this bank of words and images to compose a few sentences that describe the setting and atmosphere. Share some; identify and discuss ways in which the descriptions could be more vivid and evocative.

Group and independent work

Children use a mind map to generate and record words, similes and metaphors to describe the setting(s) for the story they are developing.

Differentiation

Low Attainers – Draw a picture of the setting for their story; annotate with descriptive words and similes.

High Attainers – Encourage children to use words and imagery to evoke mood and atmosphere.

Whole class

Ask some children to share their words, similes and metaphors; ask others to say what pictures and ideas this creates in their mind's eye.

Prompt children to extend and refine their vocabularies by focusing on different meanings and associations of synonymous words.

(NOTE Tell the children that they will now go on to draft their stories, drawing on plans and notes made in the preceding lessons. Organise time and space for this, making use of ICT where possible. Explain also that you would like them to keep a record of their attempts at words they were not sure how to spell.)

Lesson 5

Whole class

During the drafting process, choose (with their authors' permission) interesting and/or problematic pieces of writing related to development of plot, description of character and setting. If possible display them as enlarged texts. Read them together. Identify what works well and what could be improved. Discuss ways in which this might be done; look for opportunities to revisit strategies and language issues from previous lessons.

Focus in on spelling. Ask children to contribute words that they were not sure how to spell and to explain the strategies they used in attempting them. Write up and analyse the attempts, and confirm the correct spelling. Draw attention to relevant letter strings, rules, and aspects of word derivation.

Group and independent work

Children share their completed story drafts with peers and/or with you; discuss strengths and weaknesses, and possibilities for improvement, considering both content and style. Then revise as appropriate. Identify and correct spelling errors.

Differentiation

Low Attainers – Develop and polish key passages in their story.

High Attainers – Encourage children to focus on style and effect, e.g. *vividness of description, creation of suspense.*

Whole class

Share first and second drafts. Identify and discuss what has been changed and how.

Write up some mis-spellings; identify the nature and probable cause of each error.

Theme 6) Linked poems

Objectives

Text level:
- 2 to discuss how linked poems relate to one another
- 4 to comment critically on the overall impact of a poem
- 7 to annotate passages in detail
- 12 to compare texts in writing
- 13 to write a sequence of linked poems

Sentence level:
- 3 to revise formal styles of writing
- 4 to secure control of complex sentences

Word level:
- 7 to experiment with language (similes and metaphors)

Resources

Texts of sequences of linked poems, *e.g. 'A Haiku Bestiary'*

by Sandra Willingham; Ted Hughes's 'What is the Truth?' or 'Moon Whales' collections; poems beginning 'Ever ...' in Roger McGough's 'An Imaginary Menagerie', Dick King-Smith's 'Alphabeasts'. Enlarged text versions of extracts from these.
Copymasters 51 and 52, Homework 26

Assessment

At the end of this theme is the pupil able to:
- identify and discuss how poems in sequences are linked by features of content, treatment and style;
- analyse and evaluate a sequence of poems, orally and in writing;
- write a detailed comparison of two poems;
- write complex sentences in which ideas are clearly related?

Lesson 1

Whole class

Explain that in this unit the children will be reading and writing sequences of linked poems.
Read the first two or three parts of a sequence of linked poems to the children, without showing the text. Ask them to share initial ideas with a partner. Then discuss as a whole class, focusing attention on aspects that link poems in the sequence.
Show enlarged text of all or part of the poem and write up headings such as content, form, style, mood. Ask children to identify and discuss linking elements in more detail, under these headings.
Read the rest of the poem together; discuss how the links are continued and/or varied.
Ask children to think about the impact of the poem, and how they respond to it. Give them a few minutes to share ideas with a partner or to jot down ideas.
Discuss together. Model and prompt use of evaluative

language, *e.g. commenting on what is successful, powerful, effective.* Draw up two columns headed 'points' and 'evidence'; ask children to refer to the text to illustrate and support ideas; record.

Group and independent work

Children read a sequence of linked poems, and write a concise but detailed evaluation, commenting on the impact of the poem and their personal response to it.

Differentiation

Low Attainers – Write an evaluation of the poem read and discussed in whole-class work
High Attainers – Ask children to provide textual evidence for their points.

Whole class

Ask two or three children to read their evaluations; ask others to comment on views expressed and whether they have been backed up.
Identify and write up effective ways to referring to the text.

Lesson 2

Whole class

Read together an enlarged text version of another linked sequence of poems. Give pairs of children their own copy, and ask them to re-read the poem.
As in Lesson 1, prompt them to identify one or two linking elements. Talk through and model how the text of the poem can be annotated to show this.
Organise children to work in pairs, annotating their text of the poem to show and explain elements that link parts in the sequence.
Share ideas, under headings as before; look for opportunities to reinforce and extend understanding of ways in which poets manipulate words to produce effects, *e.g. through rhyme, rhythm, word choice, figurative language, breaking or bending the usual structure of sentences.*

Focus in at word level, identifying ways in which poems in the sequence are linked by patterns in vocabulary and imagery. Write up lists of words.

Group and independent work

Children write a detailed analysis of language structures in one of the two poems discussed in whole-class work, or of another sequence of linked poems.

Differentiation

Low Attainers – Give children a framework of headings to write under, matched to style of poem discussed.
High Attainers – Work from scratch to write an analysis of another sequence of linked poems.

Whole class

Choose one of the poems analysed. Ask children to share ideas about a significant element of its style.
Repeat for other poems.

Lesson 3

Whole class

Give children a few minutes to read the notes they have made about linked poems in the previous lessons. Ask them to identify points of comparison between two of these poems: what is similar about them? what is different? Share ideas.

Record similarities and differences in two columns of matched points for poem A and poem B (Copymaster 51). Explain that they will be going on to write a comparison of two linked sequences of poems. Discuss ways in which this might be organised, *e.g. poem by poem, language issue by language issue.*

Choose one clear point of comparison, and ask children to write one sentence about it on their whiteboards. Share contributions. Explain that the focus here is on relating ideas. Talk through and model connectives which have this function, *e.g. Unlike ...;... but ...; Although....* This is also an ideal context for revising the use of semi-colons to balance and relate ideas in sentences: *Poem A ...; Poem B....*

Group and independent work

Children use Copymaster 51 to record similarities and differences in relation to aspects of poetic style in two sequences of linked poems. Then draw on this to write a comparison.

Differentiation

Low Attainers – Copymaster 52. A writing frame to structure comparison of two poems.
High Attainers – Encourage children to write in the appropriate impersonal style and to refer to the text.

Whole class

Monitor independent work to select pieces of writing which illustrate issues of text organisation and sentence structure. Share these with the class, reinforcing teaching points.

Write up and analyse sentences in which structure, connectives and punctuation are used to indicate the relationships between ideas.

Lesson 4

Whole class

Return to the linked poems discussed in Lessons 1 and 2. Recap how the poems in each sequence are linked in content, form and style. Identify ways in which these could be used as a model for their own writing, *e.g. writing more poems in the sequence or a sequence about another subject in the same form.* Decide on one possibility, and use shared writing techniques to compose a new poem for the sequence, staying close to the original. Discuss other possibilities for linked poems. First, identify suitable subjects, *e.g. seasons or months of the year, animals, colours, fruits.* Then consider forms and styles, focusing on familiar short forms, *e.g. haiku, cinquains, tankas, limericks, riddles, four-line stanzas, list poems.* Decide on a subject and a form to experiment with together. Ask children (individually or in pairs) to try writing a poem for the sequence. Share some contributions, and develop them together.

Group and independent work

Children work in groups to choose a subject and form for a sequence of linked poems and plan the sequence. They then share out the work with individuals drafting poems for the sequence.

Differentiation

Low Attainers – Write in one of the simpler forms, *e.g. list poems, haiku.*
High Attainers – Write in one of the more challenging forms; focus on elements of form and style that link the poems.

Whole class

Ask groups to read some or all of their sequence to the class. Ask others to identify and comment on what links the poems.

Lesson 5

Whole class

With the authors' permission, prepare an enlarged text version of one of the sequences drafted in the previous lesson. Read and re-read together.

Lead a whole class discussion focused on issues from Lesson 1 (the overall impact of the poem) and Lesson 2 (how words are chosen and manipulated, looking in particular at elements that link poems in the sequence). Ask children (including the authors) to note down aspects of the poem that work well and others that could be improved. Share ideas; mark up and annotate the draft as appropriate. Experiment with rewriting, *e.g. pooling more powerful, exact words; strengthening linking elements.* If there is time, repeat with another sequence.

Group and independent work

Ask children to swap their drafts with another group, and to read and comment on them, identifying four areas for improvement. Return drafts to their authors for revision and completion. This offers an opportunity for extended writing, across other literacy hours or outside this context.

Differentiation

Low Attainers – 'Mark' drafts before the lesson, indicating issues to concentrate on in discussion and revision.
High Attainers – Annotate the text in detail before revising it; encourage children to address all the relevant issues.

Whole class

Return poems to groups who commented on them. Give them a few minutes to read old and new versions, and then to share comments on how effective the revision has been, quoting improvements.

Theme 7) Range of non-fiction texts

Objectives

Text level:
- 16 to identify the key features of impersonal language
- 19 to review a range of non-fiction text types and their characteristics
- 20 to secure control of impersonal writing
- 21 to divide whole texts into paragraphs
- 22 to select the appropriate style and form to suit a specific purpose and audience

Sentence level:
- 1 to revise language conventions and grammatical features of different types of text
- 3 to revise formal styles of writing

Resources
A collection of different kinds of non-fiction texts, exemplifying the characteristic features of each.

Enlarged text version of extracts from these, and of a text incorporating more than one text type. Copymasters 53 and 54, Homework 57

Assessment
At the end of this theme is the pupil able to:
- distinguish and discuss the characteristic purposes, language conventions and grammatical features of a range of non-fiction text types;
- identify the grammatical features of impersonal styles of writing and comment on their appropriateness for particular purposes;
- select non-fiction text types suitable for a range of purposes;
- plan and write a non-chronological report, organising the text in well-focused paragraphs and writing in the appropriate style?

Lesson 1

Whole class

Explain that in this theme the children will be reviewing different kinds of non-fiction texts, and planning and writing a non-chronological report.

Read aloud to the class short extracts from the two kinds of chronologically organised text: instructions and recounts. Prompt children to identify and name each; if necessary confirm and explain the terminology.

Ask children how they could tell; draw attention to relevant aspects of content, purpose and organisation. Ask children to identify and list contexts in which they have met other examples of these kinds of writing. Draw out the idea of 'appropriateness'; of the match between text-type and purpose.

Display, in turn, enlarged texts in each of these text types. Ask children, working in pairs, to identify one feature of text organisation and one of sentence structure. Share ideas. Mark up and annotate the texts to show typical features.

Group and independent work
Set three subjects for writing, e.g. *recount of familiar incident in history; recount of school event; how to make a cup of tea.* Ask children to write about each, choosing and using the appropriate style and form.

Differentiation
Low Attainers – Copymaster 53. Match text to genre title; continue writing two texts in the appropriate style.
High Attainers – Switch genres, e.g. *writing a narrative about making a cup of tea.*

Whole class
Share a text of each type. Ask children to identify characteristic features used and not used; compare with enlarged texts. Develop discussion of match between style and purpose.

Lesson 2

Whole class

In this lesson the focus is on non-chronological forms. Write up reports, explanatory texts, persuasive texts and discursive texts as titles. Give pairs of children short extracts from each of these four kinds of writing, each labelled with a letter of the alphabet. Ask them to match text and genre title.

Share answers and reasons: What is text A? How can you tell? As in Lesson 1, draw attention to content, purpose and organisation, and prompt children to identify contexts in which they have met these kinds of non-fiction writing.

Display enlarged text versions of each text-type, and as before ask children to identify features of text organisation and sentence structure. Mark up and annotate the texts to show defining characteristics.

Ask children to list the connectives in each text; to look at each list and say what they notice: What kind of connectives are typical of each? What is their function?

Group and independent work
Find in the collection of non-fiction books a short example of each of the four text types; write a definition of each and illustrate it with a typical, representative sentence.

Differentiation
Low Attainers – Give children short extracts of each type to name; then annotate to show typical features.
High Attainers – Write an explanatory caption to accompany an extract from each text type.

Whole class
Ask children to read out sentences without saying what kinds of writing they are. Ask others to identify, explaining how they can tell. Develop discussion of characteristic features, and of variation within each text type.

Lesson 3

Whole class

In this lesson, children explore non-chronological reports in more detail.

Return to the enlarged text for this genre, or choose another. Give pairs of children a copy of it to work with. Ask them to read it carefully, and note features at text, sentence and word levels that indicate it is a non-chronological report. You could support this by writing up prompts, e.g. content? sequence of paragraphs? tense? connectives? author's voice?

Share ideas. Mark up and annotate the text to show characteristic features.

At text level, work with the children to draw up a retrospective plan for the piece, identifying the focus or 'topic sentence' of each paragraph; consider their ordering.

At sentence level, focus on the features of the formal style of writing; identify absence of personal voice, use of simple present tense and passive verbs, complex sentences reflecting complex relationships in the content.

Group and independent work

Children find, in the collection of non-fiction books, another example of this text type; identify and describe a typical feature at text, sentence and word levels; write a retrospective plan.

Differentiation

Low Attainers – Give children a text to highlight and label: one colour for typical features; another for the topic of each paragraph.

High Attainers – Write a commentary on the extent to which this piece exemplifies the conventions of the genre.

Whole class

Display enlarged text version of an extract in which non-fiction styles are mixed (e.g. historical narrative incorporating elements of explanation and/or report). Ask children what they notice; identify passages of different kinds; discuss why they are used.

Lesson 4

Whole class

Discuss recent curriculum work that could be shared by writing a non-chronological report. Tease out the idea of appropriateness, emphasising the purposes of this kind of writing, especially for organising information about a general subject (e.g. all bridges, not a particular one). Agree on a topic to develop as a shared text. Write the name of the topic in the middle of the board; ask for and record contributions about major aspects of it. Taking each of these in turn, ask for and record related information. Build up a concept map (web diagram).

Talk through and demonstrate how this can be used as the basis of a plan for a non-chronological report, e.g. using main ideas as focuses for sections or paragraphs. Discuss possibilities for ordering these sections or paragraphs. Decide what needs to be added as introduction and conclusion.

Group and independent work

Children choose a subject to write a non-chronological report on; use a concept map to organise ideas; use Copymaster 54 to draw up a paragraph plan for the piece.

Differentiation

Low Attainers – Develop the piece planned in whole class work; or go straight to paragraph planning.

High Attainers – Refine their planning by organising the piece in sections consisting of linked paragraphs.

Whole class

Ask children to report back on the planning process. Which strategies worked well for them? Were there any problems?

Share and discuss some plans, focusing on how information has been organised.

Lesson 5

Whole class

Display the concept map and paragraph plan from Lesson 4. Develop and confirm content for the introductory paragraph and the following paragraph. Ask children to compose (individually or in pairs) a short introduction and an opening sentence for the next paragraph. After a few minutes, ask for contributions; develop by asking: Has anyone found a different way of saying that?

Drawing on these contributions, use shared writing techniques to draft the first two paragraphs of the report. Identify characteristic sentence level features highlighted in previous lessons.

Check that the content of the second paragraph is sharply focused round the main idea.

Group and independent work

Children write a non-chronological report, based on the plan drawn up in Lesson 4. This provides an opportunity for extended writing in further literacy hours in which you revisit the key teaching points, and/or outside this context.

Differentiation

Low Attainers – Write just two or three sections from their plan, focusing on use of typical features.

High Attainers – Monitor writing; encourage children to sustain and develop use of characteristic features.

Whole class

Share work in progress, if possible displaying some as enlarged texts. Identify and discuss organisation of the report (is it clear?) and the use of characteristic sentence and word level features.

Theme 8) Reference texts

Objectives

Text level:
- 17 to appraise a text quickly and effectively; retrieve information from it
- 18 to secure the skills of skimming, scanning and efficient reading
- 22 to select the appropriate style and form to suit a specific purpose

Sentence level:
- 3 to revise formal styles of writing

Word level:
- 3 to use independent spelling strategies: dictionaries and IT spell-checks
- 6 to practise and extend vocabulary

Resources
A collection of different kinds of reference texts on different subjects, including dictionaries, thesauruses, dictionaries of synonyms, rhyming dictionaries, encyclopaedias both general and on specific topics. Enlarged text extracts from some of these. Copymasters 55 and 56, Homework 28

Assessment
At the end of this theme is the pupil able to:
- identify the content, purpose and organisation of a range of reference texts;
- evaluate the usefulness of a reference text for a particular purpose, considering both the quality of its information and the way it is organised;
- use a range of appropriate reading strategies to locate information in reference texts;
- use formal styles to write encyclopaedia or dictionary entries?

Lesson 1
Whole class

Explain that in this theme the children will be exploring a variety of different kinds of reference texts. In preparation for this, organise a display of such texts. Choose a reference text; talk to the children about its content and purpose, and about how the information in it is organised and presented, and how it is intended to be used. Read an enlarged text extract, and identify and explain language and organisational features.

Give pairs or small groups of children a reference text to browse and discuss, focusing on the issues you have raised. After about five minutes, ask two or three groups to tell the rest of the class about the reference text they have been looking at. Draw out and develop the key issues. Focus in particular on different ways in which information is organised (alphabetical, thematic, chronological), layout (e.g. headings and sub-headings), language styles and conventions, and use of illustrations.

Group and independent work
In same groups, children write an explanatory label for their reference text, focusing on issues discussed in whole-class work. Choose a representative and interesting page at which to open the book.

Differentiation
Low Attainers – Copymaster 56. Make notes under headings indicating significant issues.
High Attainers – Encourage children to focus on language styles and conventions.

Whole class
Ask two groups to open their reference texts at the chosen page and read their 'labels'. Ask others to identify and comment on similarities and differences between the two. Discuss ways in which books in the display could be reorganised and categorised. Write labels showing this.

Lesson 2
Whole class

Give pairs of children a sophisticated dictionary. Ask them to open it at the same page, and write down all the kinds of information which the entries provide. *e.g. spelling, definition, word class, style markers (e.g. colloquial), etymology, derived words, illustrative sentence, idiomatic phrases.* Share and discuss; write a list.

Talk through and demonstrate strategies for finding a word, *e.g. using guide words to find the right page, then scanning headwords.*

Ask questions which prompt children to find different kinds of information about words.

Discuss what you need to know to find a word in the dictionary (its initial letter(s)) and difficulties that this presents with some words, *e.g. pneumonia, gnome, chaos, onion.* Ask children to suggest others.

Talk through issues in the use of spell-checks, in particular misspellings that will not be picked up (most proper nouns, misspellings that are correct spellings of other words).

Group and independent work
Children set a dictionary quiz, including questions of the kinds asked in whole-class work. Display a list of kinds of information provided by dictionaries for reference.

Differentiation
Low Attainers – Set quiz questions for children to answer, perhaps also using a simpler dictionary.
High Attainers – Write a text including mis-spellings which would not be picked up by a spell-check.

Whole class
Ask children to select their trickiest or most interesting question to ask the rest of the class, who search their dictionaries for the answer.
Reinforce and extend understanding of information in dictionaries and strategies for finding it.

Lesson 3
Whole class

In this lesson the focus is on other language reference texts.

Distribute copies of the thesauruses in use in the class (or photocopies of pages from them). Give children a couple of minutes to work out exactly how they are organised; then ask them to explain for each text. Draw attention to the overall organisation of words (alphabetical or thematic; if thematic, what kind of categories); organisation within each headword (e.g. for different fields of meaning, *e.g. for hard: difficult, firm, etc*). Identify kinds of information provided, *e.g. word list, definitions, illustrative sentences*. Discuss usefulness of each approach.

Ask children to use their thesauruses to find alternatives for specific words, answering orally or on a whiteboard. Use similar strategies to investigate the content, purpose and organisation of other language reference texts, *e.g. dictionaries of synonyms, rhyming dictionaries*.

Group and independent work
Ask children to write an entry for each of the language reference texts discussed, modelling it on the structure and content of the original. Then compare with that entry in the reference text.

Differentiation
Low Attainers – Give children a list of suitable and accessible words to work with for each text.
High Attainers – Copymaster 55. Write an entry from a dictionary of synonyms explaining the difference in meaning and use of closely related words.

Whole class
Share some of the entries written. Prompt children to say how close they got to the original entries in content and organisation.

Lesson 4
Whole class

Choose an encyclopaedia. As in Lesson 1, explain its content, purpose and organisation. Read an extract (if possible displaying it as an enlarged text); identify and discuss language features and layout.

Ask children to suggest questions which the encyclopaedia should answer. Choose one.

Talk through and demonstrate the reading strategies involved in seeking the answer: *e.g. using the structure of the book to find the right section; scanning this, e.g. by looking for key words; close reading to find information that answers the question*. Identify and discuss features of the text which make this easy/less easy.

Develop this by discussing strategies for pursuing the line of enquiry, *e.g. reading other sections to answer new questions raised*.

Identify and if possible demonstrate strategies for using reference sources on CD Rom, focusing on the same issues and strategies.

Group and independent work
Organise groups to work with print or CD Rom encyclopaedias. Ask them to pose three questions and look for answers in the encyclopaedia. Write a critical appraisal of the encyclopaedia, considering organisation and quality of information.

Differentiation
Low Attainers – Children answer two questions set by you; then pose one of their own.
High Attainers – Use the encyclopaedia to pursue a line of enquiry rather than answer individual questions.

Whole class
Ask children to report back on how they went about answering their questions and to share their appraisals of the encyclopaedia.
Revisit issues of organisation and reading strategies.

Lesson 5
Whole class

In this lesson the focus is on writing entries for reference texts, having fun with unconventional subjects.

Together, choose a science fiction or fantasy novel which creates a new world. Explain that they are going to write entries for an encyclopaedia that provides information about this world. List aspects, *e.g. invented places, creatures, machines*. Choose one and share ideas about it. Give children time out to compose a sentence for the encyclopaedia entry.

Share contributions, drawing attention to the language conventions and grammatical features of the appropriate impersonal style.

Use shared writing techniques to develop the entry.

Use similar strategies to write entries for a 'fun' language reference text, *e.g. a dictionary of currently fashionable words, providing the different kinds of information* identified in Lesson 2; a thesaurus or dictionary of synonyms for words they use to express approval or disapproval.

Group and independent work
Children work in groups to write entries for reference texts based on ideas from whole-class work. This provides an opportunity for extended writing in further Literacy Hours and/or outside this context.

Differentiation
Low Attainers – Write other entries for the 'new world' encyclopaedia begun in whole-class work.
High Attainers – Refer back to texts to write entries closely modelled on them.

Whole class
Share entries from texts of different kinds. Discuss extent to which they follow the conventions of the original texts; identify ways in which they can be improved.

Theme 9) Reviews

Objectives

Text level:
- 1 to describe and evaluate the style of an individual writer
- 9 to write summaries of books or parts of books
- 10 to write a brief synopsis of a text
- 11 to write a brief helpful review tailored for real audiences
- 22 to select the appropriate style and form to suit a specific purpose and audience

Sentence level:
- 3 to revise formal styles of writing

Word level:
- 6 to practise and extend vocabulary

Resources

A collection of reviews from magazines and newspapers, *e.g. of children's books, television programmes, films.* Large text versions of some of these, chosen to illustrate language points highlighted in lessons below. A selection of familiar novels and short stories.
Copymasters 57 and 58, Homework 29

Assessment

At the end of this theme is the pupil able to:
- identify and comment on content and language conventions of reviews;
- write a concise, accurate summary of a novel or short story;
- write a clear, accurate synopsis of the plot of a novel or short story;
- write a review of a novel or short story, evaluating and commenting on significant elements;
- identify audience needs and interests, and take account of them in their writing;
- use both personal and impersonal styles in a piece of writing?

Lesson 1

Whole class

Explain that in this theme the children will be reading and analysing reviews, and working towards writing one of their own.
Ask children to share ideas about the contexts in which they have met reviews, and to suggest features of content and style. Write up key points.
Read an enlarged text version of a review. Give children (working individually or in pairs) a couple of minutes to re-read, and to jot down what they notice under headings for content, style, audience. Share ideas; develop and refine a list of points on the board.
Focus on sentence-level features of the review. Recap features of personal and impersonal style, and ask children to identify examples of each. Review the language features of these two styles, and discuss why both can be appropriate in this kind of writing.

Group and independent work

Children read and write about another review, commenting on the issues discussed in whole-class work. Display the list of headings and other features for them to refer to.

Differentiation

Low Attainers – Copymaster 57. Read, annotate and answer questions about a book review.
High Attainers – Copymaster 58. Read, analyse and evaluate a more challenging review.

Whole class

Ask children to read a short review and their commentary on it. Develop discussion of features of reviews begun in whole-class work.
Identify, write up and analyse examples of sentences in personal and impersonal styles.

Lesson 2

Whole class

Choose a familiar short story or novel to use over the next three lessons as the subject of summary, synopsis and review.
Explain that in this lesson they will work together to write a summary of the story. Explain the meaning of this term, emphasising that a summary 'sums up' the essential features and qualities of something; that in this context the focus is on what the story is about and what it is like, rather than what happens. If possible, read a summary of another novel, *e.g. from a blurb or text inside the front cover.*
Give children time to compose a few sentences that summarise the story. Share contributions. Decide whether they do in fact serve this purpose, distinguishing between summary and synopsis.
Use shared writing strategies to compose a summary, drawing on sentences and ideas contributed.

Group and independent work

Children choose a familiar novel or short story that they find interesting, and write a summary of it. Five minutes before the end of the session, ask children to read what they have written and check that it is a summary not a re-telling.

Differentiation

Low Attainers – Limit the scale of the task by asking children to summarise a short story or picture book.
High Attainers – Start by making notes about the essential qualities of the story, considering it from different angles.

Whole class

Ask some children to read their summaries without revealing the title of the story. Ask others if they can work it out. Identify the information that indicated this most clearly.

Lesson 3

Whole class

Set the task for this lesson: to write a synopsis of the story. Explain the meaning of the term in this context (a plot precis) and distinguish it from summary. Read examples, *e.g. from blurbs, catalogue entries, inside cover copy.* Explain that these do not usually reveal the ending of the story.

Ask children to imagine that they have 30 seconds to tell someone what happens in this story: What would they say? Give them a few minutes to think about this and to make notes.

Invite two or three children to have a try. Compare their attempts, discussing differences in content (what events were included) and how they retold them in very brief terms.

Use shared writing techniques to compose a summary, drawing on these contributions.

Read it together; identify ways in which it could be improved and further shortened while still remaining accurate and informative.

Group and independent work

Children write a synopsis of the story they have chosen for use as a back cover blurb. Five minutes before the end of the session, ask children to read their synopsis and look for ways of shortening it further.

Differentiation

Low Attainers – Write a synopsis of the first episode of the story only; then shorten it further.

High Attainers – Write a blurb which will also get readers interested in the story.

Whole class

Ask some children to read their synopses/blurbs without revealing the title of the story. Ask others if they can work it out.

Share blurbs intended to entice readers; identify and discuss strategies for this.

Lesson 4

Whole class

Explain that they will now plan, write and revise a book review that will be useful and interesting for a particular audience. Together, choose a 'real' audience for these reviews, *e.g. younger children or a parallel class.* Discuss what this audience would want and need from a book review. Write up key ideas.

Discuss possible content for a book review by recapping elements of fiction *e.g. plot, setting, character, theme, atmosphere.* Discuss how this might guide their planning; identify what they might need to add as introduction and conclusion.

Use shared writing techniques to draft an introduction and a section of the review focused on an element of fiction. Draw attention to sentence-level issues discussed in Lesson 1, especially the use of personal and/or impersonal styles. Demonstrate and discuss sentences of both kinds.

Group and independent work

Children plan a review of the book they have been working on independently. They then draft it, drawing on summaries and synopses written in Lessons 2 and 3. This offers an opportunity for extended writing, across other literacy hours or in outside this context.

Differentiation

Low Attainers – Write to a framework of headings, related to elements of fiction highlighted in whole-class work.

High Attainers – Ask children to include reference to the style and structure of the story.

Whole class

Monitor work in progress; select examples for sharing and discussion which illuminate issues discussed. Use to refocus the work, and to set targets, *e.g. including comments on style, expressing a personal view.*

Lesson 5

Whole class

Return to the shared text review drafted in the previous lesson. Write up key questions: Is it useful? Interesting? What does it include/not include? How could it be improved? Does it meet the needs of the intended audience? Give children a few minutes to share ideas about each of these questions with a partner, then discuss as a class.

Identify ways in which the review could be improved and developed, and use shared writing techniques to revise it. Prepare a large text version of extracts from the children's draft reviews. Read them together. Highlight and discuss words chosen to describe the qualities of the book and the reviewer's response to it, *e.g. exciting, good, interesting.* Ask children to jot down other words that would be more exact and informative.

Group and independent work

Children re-read their drafts, considering the key questions and word choice. Then revise and develop their reviews.

Differentiation

Low Attainers – Write a revised version of just one or two sections of their review.

High Attainers – Help children to focus on the balance between personal and impersonal writing.

Whole class

Ask some children to share their first and final drafts, describing what they changed and why.

Discuss how the reviews could be organised and made available to their intended audience, *e.g. as cards in a box file, pages in a loose-leaf binder or computer data base.*

Theme 10) Study of an individual poet

Objectives:

Text level:
- 3 to describe and evaluate the style of an individual poet
- 4 to comment critically on the overall impact of a poem
- 5 to compare and contrast the work of a single writer
- 7 to annotate passages in detail
- 11 to write a brief helpful review for real audiences

Sentence level:
- 3 to revise formal styles of writing

Word level:
- 6 to practise and extend vocabulary

Resources
A collection of poems by a single poet, preferably one whose work displays marked variety in style and/or subject matter, e.g. Ted Hughes, Charles Causley, Richard Edwards, Brian Patten, Judith Nicholls. You could use published single-poet collections and poems selected from anthologies, including ones published in big book format.
Copymasters 59 and 60, Homework 30

Assessment
At the end of this theme is the pupil able to:
- identify and comment on the key features and the effect of a particular poem;
- identify and comment on the characteristic styles and concerns of an individual poet, noting the range and variety within his/her work;
- write a review of a particular poem or the work of a poet in an appropriate style and considering the needs of the intended audience;
- consider word choice in analysing poems and in writing reviews?

Lesson 1
Whole class

Explain to the children that in this theme they will be studying the work of one poet, and writing a review of one of his/her poems.
Choose a poem, and read it to the class. Re-read it, asking the children to jot down words and phrases that catch their attention and to record their impressions in notes or quick sketches. They could use notepads or small whiteboards.
Display the enlarged text of the poem, using a big book, OHT, photocopy or handwritten version, and re-read it with the children.
Ask them to share their ideas about its meaning, structure and language, drawing on their notes.
Encourage them to comment on the choice of words, considering precise meanings and impact. Write up a list of interesting or unusual words.

Group and independent work
Children read and discuss other poems by the poet. Ask them to note down key features, and to list interesting or powerful words and phrases.
Ask them to prepare and rehearse a reading aloud performance of the poem.

Differentiation:
Low Attainers – Copymaster 59. To help children focus discussion of a poem and record their ideas.
High Attainers – Give children a challenging poem; pose questions which prompt them to probe the text more deeply.

Whole class
Ask children to introduce their poem, commenting on key features and interesting word choices; and to read it aloud. List and discuss interesting vocabulary. Note down comments on the style of the poems (and keep them for use in the next lesson).

Lesson 2
Whole class

Choose a poem by the poet which contrasts with the one read in Lesson 1. Prepare an enlarged text in which some interesting or powerful words are covered.
Read the poem to the children; prompt them to consider what the 'missing' words might be. Reveal and discuss the meaning and impact of the chosen words.
Re-read the complete text. Ask the children to share impressions and questions with a partner.
Share ideas and responses all together.
As the discussion develops, prompt children to identify and comment on the poem's style and its impact. Jot down their comments.
Return to the notes on the style of the poem read in Lesson 1. Ask children what similarities and differences they can see between the two poems.

Group and independent work
Children read another poem by the poet. Ask them to identify and note down similarities and differences between this and the poem studied in Lesson 1. These could be recorded in two columns or using a Venn diagram.

Differentiation:
Low Attainers – Compare and contrast the poem they studied in Lesson 1 with one examined in whole-class work.
High Attainers – Compare all the poems read in the unit; or compare two poems, focusing on particular features, e.g. structure, tone.

Whole class
Ask children to describe features shared by the poems they have read. Use this as the starting point for defining characteristics of the poet's work. Prompt them to describe these precisely; write them up as a list.

Lesson 3

Whole class

Choose another poem by the poet, or return to one examined in Lesson 1 or 2.

Display the text so that there is space around it for annotation, *e.g. in the centre of a whiteboard or OHT.* (If possible also create space between the lines.)

Read the poem with the children, using strategies from the previous lessons. Ask them to identify and comment on features such as structure, rhyme scheme, rhythm, word choice, use of imagery.

Model how to record these features by annotating the text, *e.g. underlining and/or circling words and phrases, perhaps in different styles for different purposes;* by writing comments in the margins.

Group and independent work

Give children the text of a poem (new or from Lessons 1 or 2) and a list of questions or key words which prompt them to examine different aspects of it; ask them to annotate the text, applying techniques from whole-class work. If possible, give children enlarged texts or OHTs to work with so that annotations can be shared.

Differentiation:

Low Attainers – Children focus on just one or two suggested features, *e.g. rhyming words, images, powerful words.*

High Attainers – Children work more independently, considering a wider range of features.

Whole class

Ask children to share and talk through their annotated poems. What features have they highlighted or commented on? How?

Help the class to work together to annotate another poem; for example, two children could mark up the text at the suggestion of others.

Lesson 4

Whole class

Encourage children to discuss the general features and purposes of a review. How could these be applied to a review of a poem? How might such a review be organised? An introduction followed by paragraphs focusing on different features: structure, rhythm imagery … Who might read it?

Choose one of the poems studied in this unit. Use shared writing strategies to begin drafting a review. Prompt children to focus on aspects of language as well as content. Prompt them to move on from a first-person approach in which personal views are expressed (I like the …) to a more impersonal style in which the poem is described, analysed and evaluated (The poet uses rhythm to convey …). Prompt them also to consider what their chosen audience might want and need to know.

Group and independent work

Children draft a review of the poem from the previous lessons which they found most interesting and enjoyable.

Differentiation:

Low Attainers – Finish the review begun in the whole-class phase; write to a plan which sets out different features to be commented on.

High Attainers – Write a review comparing and contrasting two poems or of the poet's work as a whole.

Whole class

Ask children to share their draft reviews, commenting on how they have approached the task. What problems or issues have been raised for them? Look for opportunities to develop their understanding of both the poems in question and the style and organisation of a review.

Lesson 5

Whole class

Return to the shared text review begun in Lesson 4, or (with their permission) use a draft written by one of the children.

Read the draft together. Ask all the children to think of two good things about it and two ways in which it might be improved.

Share these ideas. Agree on points for improvement, and decide how to implement the changes.

Begin writing a final draft together, improving on, developing and completing the original. As the work proceeds, draw children's attention to the choice of precise and accurate words to describe features of the poem; use of an impersonal style; referring to and quoting from the text to illustrate and support points.

Group and independent work

Ask children to read and comment on each other's drafts, identifying both good points and points for improvement.

Individual children then rewrite, improving and developing their first draft.

Differentiation:

Low Attainers – Mark/annotate the children's first drafts, noting what could be changed or added; ask them to concentrate on just one or two relevant points.

High Attainers – Copymaster 60: Prompt sheet with questions which draw children's attention to the full range of issues to be considered in redrafting a review.

Whole class

Ask children who have written about the same poem to present their reviews. Discuss similarities and differences in form and content.

Develop and refine ideas about the general characteristics of the poet's work. Discuss ways of organising a class or Year Book of poetry reviews.

Word roots and origins

Sort these words into pairs with the same Latin root.
Work out what the root means.

Use a dictionary if you need help.

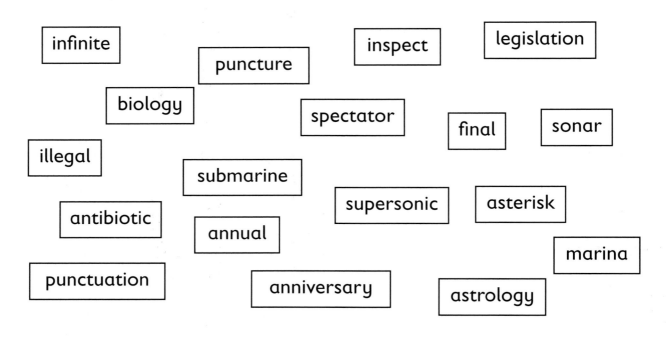

word pair	root	meaning of root

Word roots and origins

Use a dictionary to find out what countries and languages these words come from.

word	country/language
ballet	
forest	
confetti	
umbrella	
pyjamas	
shampoo	
circus	
January	
alphabet	
museum	
dock	
yacht	
skill	
husband	

Classic poetry

Make notes about a poem under these headings.

organisation of lines and verses

rhyme pattern

word choice

rhythm

metaphors and similes

What else do you notice?

Classic poetry

The Mistletoe Bough

The mistletoe hung in the castle hall,
The holly branch shone on the old oak wall;
And the baron's retainers were blithe and gay,
And keeping their Christmas holiday.
The baron beheld with a father's pride
His beautiful child, young Lovell's bride;
While she with her bright eyes seem'd to be
The star of the goodly company.

'I'm weary of dancing now,' she cried;
'Here tarry a moment – I'll hide – I'll hide!
And, Lovell, be sure thou'rt first to trace
The clue to my secret lurking place.'
Away she ran – and her friends began
Each tower to search and each nook to scan;
And young Lovell cried, 'Oh where dost thou hide?
I'm lonesome without thee, my own dear bride.'

(They look for the girl for days, for weeks, for years – but cannot find her.)

At length an oak chest, that had long lain hid,
Was found in the castle – they raised the lid –
And a skeleton form lay mouldering there,
In the bridal wreath of that lady fair!
Oh! sad was her fate! – in sportive jest
She hid from her lord in the old oak chest.
It closed with a spring! – and, dreadful doom,
The bride lay clasp'd in her living tomb!

Thomas Haynes Bayly

On another sheet of paper write a list of the 'old words' in this poem.
How would we say it now?

Set it out like this.

old word	today's version
blithe	
beheld	

Complex sentences

Fill the gaps by adding a connecting word.

Bottle gardens

When you have both plants and animals in a water garden, there is a balance. Its green weeds provide both food and oxygen for the snails. The snails breathe out carbon dioxide which the plants take up _____ they feed.

Such an arrangement can be stood near a window and left for months without attention. Check it at regular intervals to make sure the water is clear, and the plants and snails are thriving. _____ the water starts to become smelly, return the contents of the jar to the pond.

During the night, the plants slowly breathe in oxygen _____ breathe out carbon dioxide. _____ the day, _____ the light comes, the plants make food. _____ they also take in large amounts of the carbon dioxide, _____ give off large amounts of oxygen.

_____ the day especially, water from the compost is taken up by the plants and given off into the air by the leaves. It condenses on the glass _____ trickles back into the compost.

The plants were chosen _____ they do well in damp conditions. Had cacti been tried, the moisture would have injured them. Cacti are at home in dry deserts.

Plants in bottle gardens are shut off from fresh supplies of water and air and do not grow much, _____ they can last for years.

Read through the text to check that it makes sense.

Complex sentences

Here is a short, simple sentence.

Tom is my best friend.

Add a clause at the beginning.

_____ Tom is my best friend.

Add a clause in the middle.

Tom _____

_____ is my best friend.

Add a clause at the end.

Tom is my best friend _____

_____ .

Here is another simple sentence.

The explorers pitched their tents on the banks of a river.

Make a more complex sentence by adding three clauses to it: one at the beginning, one in the middle and one at the end.

_____

_____

_____

_____

_____

_____

_____

Journalistic writing

Write headlines for these traditional tales and nursery rhymes.

Goldilocks and the Three Bears

_____

The Three Billy Goats Gruff

_____

Mary had a Little Lamb

_____

The Emperor's New Clothes

_____

The Three Little Pigs

_____

Three Blind Mice

_____

Sing a Song of Sixpence

_____

Jack and the Beanstalk

_____

Journalistic writing

Imagine that you are a journalist. You have written opening sentences for two stories. Your editor has sent them back with these comments. Rewrite the sentences.

Police today claimed to have discovered important new information about the identity of the man they want to question after yesterday's theft of sand, cement, bricks and scaffolding from the site where the new supermarket is being built in Haven Road.
Too long! But you need to add information about the lorry they used.

_____

_____

_____

_____

_____

Yesterday, in front of a crowd of 15,238 people, the match between Welmouth Rovers and Welmouth City ended in a 3-all draw after two goals were disallowed and each team had a player sent off.
Make this more interesting! And say something about the weather.

_____

_____

_____

_____

_____

Make sure that you have done what your editor wanted!

Non-chronological reports

Rewrite these active sentences so that they are passive.

1. Harry broke my new pencil.

_____

2. Our teacher takes the register every morning.

_____

3. Robert scored the winning goal in extra time.

_____

4. Next, we bolted the wheels to the axle.

_____

5. Someone has eaten all my porridge!

_____

Rewrite these passive sentences so that they are active.

You might need to add some information.

1. All the sandwiches have been eaten.

_____

2. The pavements in our street are being repaired.

_____

3. A gold necklace was stolen from the palace last night.

_____

4. The plants were watered by the gardeners on hot days.

_____

5. Two pints of milk are delivered to our house every morning.

_____

Non-chronological reports

Read two or three pages from an information book. As you're reading, write down the connective you find under the correct heading.

Connectives showing order in time

_____   _____   _____

_____   _____   _____

_____   _____   _____

Connectives showing logical relationships

causes or results	contrasts or contradictions	additions and examples

Playscripts

Read this extract from a playscript. Circle the adverbs.

JAKE (*quietly but firmly*) You'd better do as I say.

SIM (*fiercely*) Why should I? Who are you to tell me what to do?

JAKE (*walks slowly towards Sim and stares threateningly into his face*) Because if you don't I'll tell your parents about the car. That's why.

SIM (*unbelievingly*) You wouldn't, would you?

Write the adverbs down in one of the lists.

Add other adverbs that can be used to describe how people talk, move and behave.

talk	move	behave

Playscripts

This is an extract from the play of Bill Naughton's famous short story, 'The Goalkeeper's Revenge'.

Sammy and Bill are flying a kite.

SAMMY: How's she been pullin', Bill?

BILL (*handing over string*): Strong. Her's been pulling strong. Can tha' feel them flecks o' rain, Sammy?

SAMMY: Aye, I thought I did feel a drop then.

BILL: Tha's better pull in then, eh?

SAMMY: I don't like having a kite up, wi'out going bare stick.

BILL: You're not letting off more, Sammy?

SAMMY: Aye! It's half-hearted else. You just watch her take it. (*Unwinds*) Only a few more yards, bare stick, then wind in.

BILL: That's enough, Sammy. (*Suddenly the string flies off and away*) The string – grab it!

They rush hopelessly – perhaps falling over

BILL: No use, Sam – it'll be falling now – miles away – like a great broken bird.

SAMMY: The last I'll ever see of her, Bill.

BILL: Ee, I'm sorry, Sammy.

SAMMY: I'll never understand how that string weren't tied on to the winding stick. I've never known it. It's the first thing I do – tie it on. I must have forgot. (*He picks up the stick*) Here, Bill. That's a good winding stick. Thee have it. (*Pause*) Go on.

What do you notice about how these characters talk?

Use this chart to record your ideas.

special or unusual words	how I would say it
Continue on another sheet	

Classic fiction on screen and in print

Use this sheet to record words and expressions that are no longer in use.

Title of book _____   Author _____

'old' words and expressions	how we would say it today

Classic fiction on screen and in print

Storyboard planning

You might need more copies of this sheet.

Shakespeare

Read this passage from *Love's Labours Lost.*

When icicles hang by the wall,
> And Dick the shepherd blows his nail;
And Tom bears logs into the hall,
> And milk comes frozen home in pail;
When blood is nipp'd, and ways be foul,
Then nightly sings the staring owl,
> Tu-whit to-who.
> > A merry note,
While greasy Joan doth keel the pot.

When all aloud the wind doth blow,
> And coughing drowns the parson's saw;
And birds sit brooding in the snow,
> And Marian's nose is red and raw:
When roasted crabs hiss in the bowl,
Then nightly sings the staring owl,
> Tu-whit to-who.
> > A merry note,
While greasy Joan doth keel the pot.

Make a list of words and phrases that are no longer in use. Try to work out what they mean, and what we would say instead now.

old words and phrases	what we say now

Shakespeare

Read this passage from Shakespeare's play *Henry IV*.
Make a list of words and phrases that are no longer in use. Try to work out what they mean, and what we would say instead now.

It is night. Henry IV, King of England, is facing a rebellion by some of his subjects; he cannot sleep.

How many thousand of my poorest subjects
Are at this hour asleep! O Sleep, O gentle sleep,
Nature's soft nurse, how have I frighted thee,
That thou no more wilt weigh my eyelids down,
And steep my senses in forgetfulness?
Why rather, sleep, liest thou in smoky cribs,
Upon uneasy pallets stretching thee,
And hush'd with buzzing night-flies to thy slumber,
Than in perfum'd chambers of the great,
Under the canopies of costly state,
And lull'd with sound of sweetest melody ...
Wilt thou upon the high and giddy mast
Seal up the ship-boy's eyes, and rock his brains
In cradle of the rude imperious surge,
And in the visitation of the winds,
Who take the ruffian billows by the top,
Curling their monstrous heads, and hanging them
With deafing clamour in the slippery clouds,
That with the hurly death itself awakes?
Canst thou, O partial sleep, give thy repose
To the wet sea-boy in an hour so rude;
And in the calmest and most stillest night,
With all appliances and means to boot,
Deny it to a king? Then, happy low, lie down!
Uneasy lies the head that wears a crown.

old words and phrases	what we say now

Continue on another sheet.

83

Viewpoint in fiction

Write two multiple choice questions about the story.
Set them out like this.

1) Question _____

_____

Tick the right answer.

☐ _____   ☐ _____

☐ _____   ☐ _____

2) Question _____

_____

Tick the right answer.

☐ _____   ☐ _____

☐ _____   ☐ _____

Write two open questions about the story.
Set them out like this. Write the answers too!

3) Question _____

_____

Answer _____

_____

4) Question _____

_____

Answer _____

_____

Viewpoint in fiction

Think about the main character in the story.

In the left hand column, write down three statements about him or her. In the right hand column, write down words from the story that support the statement.

statements about the character	evidence from the text
1)	
2)	
3)	

Biography and autobiography

Some of these extracts are from biographies; some are from autobiographies. Circle words that tell you which is which, and tick the correct box.

A biography ☐ autobiography ☐

My four friends and I had come across a loose floor-board at the back of the classroom, and when we prised it up with the blade of a pocket-knife, we discovered a big hollow space underneath. This, we decided, would be our secret hiding place for sweets and other small treasures, such as conkers and monkey nuts and birds' eggs.

B biography ☐ autobiography ☐

When he was about eight years old, Benjamin's parents were having one of their many arguments. He dashed out of the house and escaped into the street. Some marbles dropped out of a small hole in his pocket. As he crouched down to pick them up, he heard his sister scream 'Watch out, Benj!'
Benjamin shot upright, and saw a cyclist riding straight at him, one arm in the air.

C biography ☐ autobiography ☐

In 1888 Gandhi set out on the three week voyage to London where he was going to study law. He was nineteen and already a father: this first son, Harilal, had been born some months earlier.
    In London, he felt lonely, cut off from his family and home.

D biography ☐ autobiography ☐

It was a bright Sunday morning in early June, the right time to be leaving home. My three sisters and a brother had already gone before me; two other brothers had yet to make up their minds. They were still sleeping that morning, but my mother had got up early and cooked me a heavy breakfast, had stood wordlessly while I ate it, her hand on my chair, and had then helped me pack up my few belongings.

Biography and autobiography

APPLICATION FOR _____

NAME _____

ADDRESS _____

_____

_____

PRESENT OCCUPATION _____

KEY SKILLS AND EXPERIENCES

-

-

-

-

EDUCATION

_____

_____

INTERESTS AND HOBBIES

_____

_____

_____

_____

_____

Word roots and origins

Cut out these words. Sort them into families of derived words.

imagine

memorable

person

imaginative

possessive

circular

imagination

encircle

personification

impersonal

transport

portable

pleasure

possess

unimaginable

unpleasant

displease

gracefully

circle

purification

disgraceful

grace

reporter

impure

pure

memorial

memory

please

repossess

Choose one word from each family, and use it in a sentence.

1. _____

2. _____

3. _____

4. _____

Continue on another sheet.

Word roots and origins

Use a dictionary to find out the origin of these words.
Circle the part of the word which has an unusual spelling pattern.

Word	Origin
kayak	
tobacco	
yacht	
bazaar	
kiosk	
chaos	
chauffeur	
wok	
karate	
menu	
verandah	
pyjamas	
broccoli	
antique	
avalanche	
dinghy	
gymkhana	
confetti	

Commentaries

Find related words, and write them down in the charts.

Find words that

light

rhyme with	include the same letter string (gh or ght)	are derived from

knee

rhyme with	include the same letter string (kn or ee)	are derived from

bigger

rhyme with	include the same letter string (er)	follow the same spelling rule

happily

have the same root	follow the same spelling rule	include the same letter string (pp)

Commentaries

This is the beginning of a newspaper article about the voyage of the *Matthew* in 1997. It consists of four long, complex sentences.

Circle the main verb and underline the main clause in each sentence.

On June 24, five hundred years to the day after the explorer John Cabot first stepped ashore on North American soil, a replica of his boat, the *Matthew*, will land at Bonavista Point in Newfoundland, the place where John Cabot is believed to have made his landfall, having made the same transatlantic crossing from Bristol.

Cabot, or Giovanni Caboti as he was properly called, is relatively unknown compared to Christopher Columbus, who five years earlier in 1492 had discovered the 'New World' when he sailed across the Atlantic to the Caribbean. Yet Cabot is every bit as important a figure: while Columbus and his crew were still exploring the Caribbean and were unaware of the land mass that lay beyond, Cabot, sailing at much more northerly latitudes, became the first European of his generation to set foot on the North American continent. In doing so, he claimed the land for the English King, Henry VII, and was in many ways responsible for North America becoming a part of the English-speaking world.

John Crace

Fiction genres

Underline the prefix. Write two more words that begin with this prefix.

decode   _____   _____

disconnect   _____   _____

misunderstand   _____   _____

recycle   _____   _____

subtitle   _____   _____

interview   _____   _____

Underline the suffix. Write two more words that end with this suffix.

kindness   _____   _____

hopeful   _____   _____

natural   _____   _____

active   _____   _____

famous   _____   _____

tasty   _____   _____

appearance   _____   _____

creation   _____   _____

Fiction genres

In all these words a prefix and a suffix are added to the root word.
Use this chart to record the structure of these words.
Add more words with prefixes and suffixes.

word	root	prefix	suffix
disappearance			
prehistoric			
deforestation			
disgraceful			
invariable			
reexamination			
unfortunate			
inelegantly			
reemergence			

Humorous verse

Here are 20 invented words. Write down ten which are **possible** words in English.

nkell   delend   reffage   garket   tince

weach   cloater   rlonk   mrat   rable   frake

drohpi   ckast   sleem   fubbish   slpot   saot

letf   ghilprt   wint   drohpi

1 _____   2 _____

3 _____   4 _____

5 _____   6 _____

7 _____   8 _____

9 _____   10 _____

Now write more invented words of your own.

possible	impossible

Humorous verse

Work out the answers to these traditional riddles.

Black I am and much admired,
Men seek for me until they're tired;
When they find me, break my head,
And take me from my resting bed.

answer: _____

As I was walking in a field of wheat,
I picked up something good to eat;
Neither fish, flesh, fowl, nor bone,
I kept it till it ran alone.

answer: _____

Little Nancy Etticoat
With a white petticoat,
And a red nose;
She has no feet or hands,
The longer she stands
The shorter she grows.

answer: _____

Use ideas and patterns from these riddles to help you write one of
your own.

_____

_____

_____

_____

Narrative structure

This is the beginning of Betsy Byars' novel *The Eighteenth Emergency*. But there is a problem! The paragraphs have been muddled up.
Cut them out, and put them in the right order.

The two of them ran together for a block. The dog's legs were so short he appeared to be on wheels. His Cracker Jack box was hitting the sidewalk. He kept glancing at the boy because he didn't know why they were running. The boy knew. He did not even notice the dog beside him or the trail of spilled Cracker Jacks behind.

Inside the building the boy was still running. He went up the stairs three at a time, stumbled, pulled himself up by the banister and kept going until he was safely inside his own apartment. Then he sagged against the door.

The pigeons flew out of the alley in one long swoop and settled on the awning of the grocery store. A dog ran out of the alley with a torn Cracker Jack box in his mouth. Then came the boy.

His mother was sitting on the sofa, going over some papers. The boy waited for her to look up and ask him what had happened. He thought she should be able to hear something was wrong just from the terrible way he was breathing. 'Mom,' he said.

Suddenly the boy slowed down, went up some stairs and entered an apartment building. The dog stopped. He sensed that the danger had passed, but he stood for a moment at the bottom of the stairs. Then he went back to eat the Cracker Jacks scattered on the sidewalk and to snarl at the pigeons who had flown down to get some.

The boy was running hard and fast. He stopped at the sidewalk, looked both ways, saw that the street was deserted and kept going. The dog caught the boy's fear, and he started running with him.

Underline words and phrases that link the paragraphs.

Narrative structure

This is an extract from the novel *Tom's Midnight* Garden by Philippa Pearce. Underline words and phrases that indicate time. Annotate the text to show how the author handles time in this episode.

Hatty was standing there, only a few yards from him, staring at him. Then Tom – not knowing whether he was indeed speaking to ears that could hear him – said: "I knew you were hiding from me and watching me, just now."

She might have meant to pretend not to hear him; but her vanity could not resist this opening. "Just now!" she cried, scornfully. "Why, I've hidden and watched you, often and often, before this! I saw you when you ran along by the nut stubs and then used my secret hedge tunnel into the meadow! I saw you when Susan was dusting and you waved from the top of the yew tree! I saw you when you went right through the orchard door!" She hesitated, as though the memory upset her a little; but then went on. "Oh, I've seen you often – and often – and often – when you never knew it!"

So that was the meaning of the footprints on the grass, on that first day; that was the meaning of the shadowy form and face at the back of the bedroom, across the lawn; that, in short, was the meaning of the queer feeling of being watched, which Tom had had in the garden so often, that, in the end, he had come to accept it without speculation.

A kind of respect for the girl crept into Tom's mind. "You don't hide badly, for a girl," he said. He saw at once that the remark angered her, so he hurried on to introduce himself: "I'm Tom Long," he said.

Official language

Rewrite these sentences using active verbs.

1. Dirty plates should be taken to the serving hatch.

_____

2. The bell will be rung five minutes before the start of morning school.

_____

3. Classes will be called from the playground in order, from Year 3 to Year 6.

_____

4. Seat belts must be worn when the red light shows.

_____

5. All breakages must be paid for.

_____

Write a sentence with a passive verb about:

using the library

_____

_____

school uniform

_____

_____

assembly

_____

_____

Official language

These words are often used in official writing.
Write down an informal word that means more or less the same.

reside	
transpire	
commence	
envisaged	
utilise	
located	
desist	
endeavour	
purchase	
situated	
obtain	
prior to	
notify	
subsequent	
require	
in the event of	

Use a dictionary if you need to check the meaning of these words.

Poetic devices

In this poem, the poet uses the sounds of words to depict a peaceful moonlit night.

Circle words chosen to create this effect.

Find and underline a line which moves more quickly. Circle the word which creates this different effect.

Silver

Slowly, silently, now the moon
Walks the night in her silver shoon;
This way, and that, she peers, and sees
Silver fruit upon silver trees;
One by one the casements catch
Her beams beneath the silvery thatch;
Couched in his kennel, like a log,
With paws of silver sleeps the dog;
From their shadowy cote the white breasts peep
Of doves in a silver-feathered sleep;
A harvest mouse goes scampering by,
With silver claws and silver eye;
And moveless fish in the water gleam,
By silver reeds in a silver stream.

Walter de la Mare

Write more words with a sleepy, peaceful sound.

_____   _____   _____

_____   _____   _____

_____   _____   _____

Poetic devices

Mark up and annotate this poem to show how the poet uses metaphors and similes to describe pigeons vividly and powerfully.

Pigeons

They paddle with staccato feet
In powder-pools of sunlight,
Small blue busybodies
Strutting like fat gentlemen
With hands clasped
Under their swallowtail coats;
And, as they stump about,
Their heads like tiny hammers
Tap at imaginary nails
In non-existent walls.
Elusive ghosts of sunshine
Slither down the green gloss
Of their necks an instant, and are gone.

Summer hangs drugged from sky to earth
In limpid fathoms of silence:
Only warm dark dimples of sound
Slide like slow bubbles
From the contented throats.

Raise a casual hand—
With one quick gust
They fountain into air.

Richard Kell

Poetic forms

Write the correct letter in the box to match the verse to the rhyme scheme.

1 aabb ☐   **2** abcb ☐
3 abab ☐   **4** aaab ☐

A

The Romans built me straight,
They knew where they were going.
I am the quickest route there is
Unless the flies are crowing.

John Mole

B

What starts the thunder overhead?
Who makes the crashing noise?
Are the angels falling out of bed?
Are they breaking all their toys?

Louis Untermeyer

C

The man in the Wilderness asked of me,
'How many strawberries grow in the salt sea?'
I answered him as I thought good,
'As many red herrings as grow in the wood.'

anon

D

Under the wide and starry sky,
Dig the grave and let me lie.
Glad did I live and gladly die,
And I laid me down with a will.

Robert Louis Stevenson

Poetic forms

Use letters of the alphabet to show the rhyme scheme of the first
verse.
Fill in the rhymes in the next three verses, following the same pattern.

Through That Door

Through that door
Is a garden with a wall,
The red brick crumbling,
The lupins growing tall,
Where the lawn is like a carpet
Spread for you,
And it's all as tranquil
As you ever knew.

Through that door
Is your secret room
Where the window lets in
The light of the _____,
With its mysteries and magic
Where you can find
Thrills and excitements
Of every _____.

Through that door
Are the mountains and the moors
And the rivers and the forests
Of the great _____,
All the plains and the ice-caps
And lakes as blue as _____
For all those creatures
That walk or swim or fly.

Through that door
Is the city of the _____
Where you can imagine
What you'll find.
You can make of that city
What you want it to,
And if you choose to share it,
Then it could come _____.

John Cotton

Proverbs

Each of these proverbs includes a word that usually has a different meaning when it is used today.
Circle that word.
Rewrite the proverb using a word that we would use instead now.

1. Empty vessels make the most noise.

_____

_____

_____

2. He that has a full purse never wanted a friend.

_____

_____

_____

3. It is an ill wind that blows nobody any good.

_____

_____

_____

4. The mouse that has but one hole is quickly taken.

_____

_____

_____

5. A thing that you don't want is dear at any price.

_____

_____

_____

Proverbs

Some of these proverbs are sentences, and some are not. Tick the box to show which is which.

	sentence	not a sentence
More haste, less speed.		
Like father, like son.		
Once bitten, twice shy.		
Never say die.		
First come, first served.		
A stitch in time saves nine.		
All work and no play makes Jack a dull boy.		
He who hesitates is lost.		
Sticks and stones may break my bones but words will never hurt me.		
The hand that rocks the cradle rules the world.		
Dead men tell no tales.		
Out of sight, out of mind.		
Much would have more.		
In for a penny, in for a pound.		

Now find and write down another proverb that is a sentence

_____

and one that is not.

_____

Look again at the proverbs that are sentences. Circle the main verb or verbs.

Arguments

Use these words to fill the gaps in the conditional sentences.

| would | will | if | could | then | might |

Cars

Today, most people use cars to get from place to place. This causes lots of problems. I think that people should use cars less. These are my reasons.

First, more and more parents take their children to school by car. _____ this goes on, _____ children _____ become less fit and _____ become ill when they grow up.

Second, more cars mean more pollution. Some scientists think that this _____ be the reason why more children have asthma. This _____ be reduced _____ cars had engines that made less fumes.

Also, it takes lots of resources to make a car, especially the big jeeps that are fashionable now. _____ we go on building more and more cars, we _____ soon run out of resources, and we _____ not have enough to make other things we need.

There are three main points in this argument.
Write a short note to say what they are.

1 _____

_____

2 _____

_____

3 _____

_____

Arguments

Write pairs of linked sentences using these connecting words and phrases.

1. similarly

_____

2. on the other hand

_____

3. as a result

_____

4. however

_____

5. meanwhile

Word play

Write four more sentences with this structure.

The old man	kicked	the football	through the window.
The black dog	chased	the milkman	down the road.
The little girl	threw	the ice-cream	into the fire.
The tall postman	pushed	the bike	up the hill.

Cut the sentences into parts, and muddle them up.
What new sentences can you make? They can be 'silly sentences'!

Word play

Complete these pairs of eye-rhymes.
Remember: the words look the same but sound different.

bead _____

one _____

low _____

have _____

great _____

shall _____

give _____

good _____

over _____

bear _____

find _____

arm _____

form _____ CLUE An animal that lives in the soil.

pour _____ CLUE The opposite of sweet.

touch _____ CLUE People can sit on this.

work _____ CLUE You eat with this.

Make up your own pairs of eye-rhymes.

_____   _____

_____   _____

_____   _____

Advertisements

Read this advertisement for cars.

A real cool offer for a hot car!

The new special edition Roma is the little car with the big, big heart.

Fun to drive in the open country.
Easy to drive round the city streets.

With the Roma you get to choose! – from 4 dazzling metallic colours.

Summer skies   Sea green   Mountain white   Golden sands

Colours that say 'The good times are here!'

The new 1.6 litre engine is a tiger!

Giving you the power and control you've always yearned for.

Stylishly finished interiors in matching colours, with driver's air-bag and integral radio/CD player.

All this makes the special edition Roma the best little car on the road.

Now available on 12 months' interest free credit.

On a separate sheet of paper write a commentary on the advertisement.

Here are some questions to get you thinking.

What are the main selling-points?
Who is the advertisement aimed at?

How does the advertisement use language?
Look at: • word choice

• sentence structure

• metaphors.

Advertisements

Read this advertisement for

Furniture Classics

Elegant designs that have stood the test of time.

Furniture that transports you to a past when life was more relaxed. More graceful.

Made from the timber of beech trees that have grown slowly to maturity in the depths of quiet woodlands.

Hand-made and hand-finished by craftsmen. Craftsmen versed in ancient skills, passed down from generation to generation.
Craftsmen who work to bring you furniture to last a lifetime and beyond.

On a separate sheet of paper write a commentary on this advertisement.
Think about:
• the main selling point
• the use of language, especially word choice.

Write an advertisement for furniture with a modern appeal.
Start by writing a list of words you could use.

Comparing novelists

Scribe's prompt sheet

As the group reads and discusses the extract, note down their ideas about:

plot

setting

characters

language

mood

themes and ideas

Comparing novelists

Here are short extracts from two novels.
Talk and make notes about the differences you can see.
Think especially about:
- style
- who's telling the story
- tone
- choice of words

Bobbie knew the secret now. A sheet of old newspaper wrapped round a parcel – just a little chance like that – had given the secret to her. And she had to go down to tea and pretend that there was nothing the matter. The pretence was bravely made, but it wasn't very successful.

For when she came in, everybody looked up from tea and saw her pink-lidded eyes and pale face with red tear-blotches on it.

'My darling,' cried Mother, jumping up from the tea-tray, 'Whatever is the matter?'

'My head aches, rather,' said Bobbie. And indeed it did.

'Has anything gone wrong?' Mother asked.

'I'm all right, really,' said Bobbie, and she telegraphed her Mother from her swollen eyes this brief, imploring message – '*Not before the others!*'

The Railway Children by E. Nesbit.

Well, here I am again, sitting outside the principal's office, And I've only been at the school for two day. Two lots of trouble in two days! Yesterday I got the strap for nothing. Nothing at all.

I see this bloke walking along the street wearing a pink bow tie. It looks like a great pink butterfly attacking his neck. It is the silliest bow tie I have ever seen. 'What are you staring at, lad?' says the bloke. He is in a bad mood.

'Your bow tie,' I tell him. 'It is ridiculous. It looks like a pink vampire.' It is so funny that I start to laugh my head off.

Nobody tells me that this bloke is Old Splodge, the Principal of the school. He doesn't see the joke and he gives me the strap. Life is very unfair.

The Pink Bow Tie by Paul Jennings

Explanatory texts

Read this explanation of how free range eggs are produced and packed.

During the day, free-range hens can wander in a field. At night they are kept inside a hen-house out of the cold and away from foxes. The hens are fed and watered inside.

The hens lay their eggs in nesting-boxes at the back of the hen-house. The eggs roll through a flap to a bench outside, where they are collected twice day.

The newly laid eggs are taken by lorry to the packing station. The eggs are passed under lights, which show up any cracks in their shells. This is called candling because the eggs were once checked by candlelight. Any cracked or broken eggs are used to make paint, soap, shampoo, ink and fertilizer.

Next, the eggs are sorted into sizes. Seven sizes of egg are sold in the shops. Size one is the biggest.

Six or twelve eggs are packed into each egg-box. The box holds the eggs safely in place so that they won't break.

Each box is date-stamped to show how fresh the eggs are. It takes only one or two days for an egg to get from the hen to the supermarket.

Mark up and annotate the text to show features of explanatory writing.

Look for: • connecting words and phrases
• passive sentences
• verbs in the present tense
• specialist vocabulary.

Explanatory texts

Use this flow-chart to make notes for writing an explanation.

Extended story

Use this chart to plan your story.

plot beginning	middle	end

setting(s)
Where does the story take place?

characters
Who's in the story? What are they like? What are the relationships between them?

Extended story

Use this chart to plan your story.

What is the situation at the start?
What happens to get the story going?
How do things develop? (note down a few important events)
What is the climax of the story?
How do things work out in the end?

Linked poems

Use this chart to compare two poems.

poem A	poem B
rhyme pattern	
rhythm	
organisation in lines and verses	
similes and metaphors	
word choice	
tone	
other features	

Linked poems

Use this writing frame to help you write a comparison of two poems.

The poems I am comparing are _____

and _____

These poems are alike in some ways. For example, they both

_____

_____

Both poems also _____

_____

Another similarity is that _____

_____

The two poems are also very different. One difference is that

_____

_____

They are also different in the way they

_____

Unlike _____

_____

Finally, _____

_____

Range of non-fiction texts

Here are five labels for different kinds of non-fiction writing.

| instructions | | non-chronological report | | explanation |

| persuasive | | recount |

Here are extracts from five non-fiction texts.

Most animals use their tongues for eating in much the same way we do. Some animals use their tongues in different ways. The chameleon has a sticky tongue which it shoots out to catch its prey. The frog also has a sticky tongue which, unlike the human tongue, is rooted at the front of its mouth.

The molten glass moves down tubes to the moulding machine. As it oozes out of the tubes, it is cut into pieces by a huge pair of mechanical scissors. Each blob of glass then moves down another tube into a mould where its shaped by air pressure.

Lay the stencil over a piece of paper. Following the shape of the stencil, spread glue on the paper. Sprinkle sand on the paper and leave the glue to dry before lifting off the stencil and shaking off excess sand.

It was a cold December. Almost as soon as the train steamed out of town, the wheels of the carriages began to slip. The brakes could not hold the heavy train. Gradually, the engine began to gather speed under the weight of the carriages. The train was running out of control. Then a new danger threatened.

We support the move to school uniforms. When children are wearing all kinds of clothes, it is difficult for teachers to keep track of them on outings. Also, if everyone is wearing a uniform, children don't waste time worrying about whether they are 'fashionably' dressed or not. As everyone knows, arguments and teasing about this cause a lot of trouble at play-times.

Cut out the labels and the texts. Match them together.
Add one more sentence to the persuasive text and the non-chronological report.

Range of non-fiction texts

Paragraph planner

paragraph 1
main idea

supporting detail
-
-
-

paragraph 2
main idea

supporting detail
-
-
-

paragraph 3
main idea

supporting detail
-
-
-

paragraph 4
main idea

supporting detail
-
-
-

Reference texts

Write entries for a dictionary of synonyms for these words.
Explain exactly how they differ in meaning.
For each word, write a sentence that illustrates its use.

angry

_____

cross

_____

annoyed

_____

bad-tempered

_____

furious

_____

grumpy

_____

Reference texts

Use this chart to make notes about a reference text.

title
content
purpose
organisation
use of illustration
language styles and features

Reviews

Read this book review written by a child.

Black Beauty
by Anna Sewell

Black Beauty is a book written from the point of view of a horse. He is a good tempered horse and experiences many kinds of owners, from nasty to nice. His owners make him do all sorts of jobs from being a carriage horse to a cab horse. There weren't many illustrations but the ones that were in it were lovely. They were quite simple but gave a good impression of the scenes described in the book.

   Two other books of the same sort are Stray by A. N. Wilson and Blitzcat by Robert Westall. Unlike Black Beauty, Stray is funny but like Black Beauty it's emotional and exciting. Blitzcat is very much like Black Beauty because it's serious and moving. All three books are written from the point of view of an animal. In my opinion Black Beauty is a brilliant book. The chosen words describe the book and its scenes perfectly. It was as if I really was looking through the eyes of a horse.

Rebecca Heron

Underline in red the parts of the review that tell you about the plot of Black Beauty.
Underline in blue the parts that tell you how the book is written.
Underline in black the parts that compare Black Beauty with other stories.
Circle words that show Rebecca's opinion about the book.

Answer these questions.

1. What is unusual about the way in which the story of Black Beauty is told?

_____

2. What is the same about Black Beauty and Stray? _____

_____

What is different? _____

3. What does Rebecca especially like about Black Beauty?

_____

4. What does she like about the illustrations?

_____

5. What is the same about all three stories that Rebecca writes about?_____

_____

Reviews

Read this review.

> **Comfort Herself**
> Geraldine Kaye, illus Jennifer Northway
>
> Superb! Eleven-year-old Comfort Kwatey-Jones is a touching and believable heroine. With a white English mother and a Ghanain father, Comfort's journey in search of herself forms the basis of this fascinating, well-written, and well-researched book. After the death of her mother in a road accident, Comfort is rocketed in a short space of time through a succession of experiences: a children's home, a Kentish village with her prim middle-class white grandparents, and urban and rural Ghana, where she goes to be reunited with the father she has not seen since she was a toddler. Despite this veritable kaleidoscope of settings and cultures, each is fully, fairly and convincingly presented, particularly the rural Ghanain village where Comfort spends six months with her paternal grandmother. An excellent book in all ways . . . Clear print, frequent good illustrations, and an attractive jacket make it visually very appealing.

List the words that show the reviewer's opinion of the book.

Answer these questions.

1. Who is the main character in the novel?

_____

2. Where is the story set?

_____

3. What do you think the reviewer means by these phrases?
a veritable kaleidoscope

_____

well-researched

_____

4. What are the strengths of this review?

_____

_____

5. How could it be improved?

_____

_____

Study of an individual poet

Read and re-read the poem.
Talk about these things in your group. Or jot down your ideas.

The main idea of the poem

Interesting or unusual words

Rhyming words and the pattern they make

Structure of verses

Rhythm

Your favourite line. What do you like about it? Why?

Questions about the poem

Study of an individual poet

Check list for revising and editing reviews of poems or of a poet's work.

Re-read your review carefully.
Have you:

- written about   word choice? ☐
         rhythm? ☐
         rhyme? ☐
         tone? ☐
         organisation of lines and verses? ☐
         sentence structures? ☐
         use of similes and metaphors? ☐
         ideas? ☐

- supported your opinions by   explaining your reasons? ☐
         referring to the detail of the text? ☐
         quoting from the poem? ☐

- organised the review clearly in well-focused paragraphs, with an introduction and conclusion? ☐

- thought about your readers   about what they know and do not know? ☐
         about what they would be interested in? ☐

Have you checked

- sentence structure   have you made your meaning clear? ☐
         are sentences grammatically correct? ☐
- punctuation   is it accurate? ☐
         does it help the reader? ☐
- spelling   look especially at
         – words you know you have trouble with ☐
         – words with irregular spellings ☐
         – word endings ☐

When you have checked – make changes to improve your review.

Word roots and origins

The literacy work this week has been concerned with the structure and origin of words. The children have investigated prefixes and suffixes from Greek (such as tele, geo, photo) and Latin (such as sub, trans, multi, ped).

As you are reading – note down
• words that you think come from Latin

_____   _____

_____   _____

_____   _____

_____   _____

• words that you think come from Greek

_____   _____

_____   _____

_____   _____

_____   _____

• other interesting words

_____   _____

_____   _____

_____   _____

_____   _____

Use a dictionary to find out about the origins of these words.

Classic poetry

In literacy work this week the children have been studying older poems. They have drafted and revised poems which use personification. At sentence level the focus has been on active and passive verbs. At word level the children have investigated how the meaning of some words has changed over time.

Record words and expressions that are no longer in use. Work out what they mean.

title of poem _____   author _____

word	meaning

Complex sentences

Literacy work this week has been concerned with the structure and punctuation of complicated sentences.

The word level focus has been on words used to link ideas in sentences, such as then, because, which, who.

Choose a text to read.

It could be
- a newspaper story
- an extract from a story
- part of a non-fiction book

Read until you have found 10 connecting words or phrases.

List them here.

_____   _____

_____   _____

_____   _____

_____   _____

_____   _____

Choose 5 of these connecting words or phrases and use each in a sentence of your own.

1 _____

_____

2 _____

_____

3 _____

_____

4 _____

_____

5 _____

_____

Journalistic writing

In literacy work this week the children have been investigating the ways in which language is used in newspapers. They have planned and written their own newspaper stories.

At sentence level the focus has been on the structure and punctuation of complex sentences.

Find and write down three interesting or unusual headlines and opening sentences in newspapers.

Write comments about how they are written.

headline	comment

opening sentence	comment

Non-chronological reports

In literacy work this week the children have been identifying the features of non-chronological reports. They have written reports about subjects they have studied in other lessons. At sentence level the focus has been on connecting words and on active and passive verbs. At word level the focus has been on the meaning and spelling of connecting words.

While you are reading a story – write down the connectives you find.

_____   _____   _____

_____   _____   _____

What do you notice? _____

_____

_____

_____

While you are reading a discursive text or argument – write down the connectives you find.

_____   _____   _____

_____   _____   _____

What do you notice? _____

_____

_____

_____

Playscripts

In literacy work this week the children have been reading playscripts and investigating how they are turned into films or television dramas. They have rewritten part of a story as a playscript. At sentence level they have been revising word classes and the conventions of Standard English.

Watch a television drama. Make notes about it under these headings. Give it star ratings (up to five).

Title of drama _____

action   STAR RATING

_____

_____

setting   STAR RATING

_____

_____

mood   STAR RATING

_____

_____

characters STAR RATING

_____

_____

dialogue   STAR RATING

_____

_____

Use your notes to help you write a review.

Classic fiction on screen and in print

In literacy work this week the children have been exploring how classic novels are adapted for film or television. They have reworked part of a story as a filmscript. At sentence level they have revised the structure of complex sentences. At word level they have investigated how the meaning of some words and expressions has changed over time.

Charles Dickens' *A Christmas Carol* was published in 1843.
Read this extract carefully.

Once upon a time – of all the good days in the year, on Christmas Eve – old Scrooge sat busy in his counting-house. It was cold, bleak, biting weather: foggy withal: and he could hear people in the court outside go wheezing up and down, beating their hands upon their breasts, and stamping their feet upon the pavement stones to warm them. The city clocks had only just gone three, but it was quite dark already: it had not been light all day: and candles were flaring in the windows of the neighbouring offices, like ruddy smears upon the palpable brown air. The fog came pouring in at every chink and keyhole, and was so dense without, that although the court was of the narrowest, the houses opposite were mere phantoms. To see the dingy cloud come drooping down, obscuring everything, one might have thought that Nature lived hard by, and was brewing on a large scale.

The door of Scrooge's counting-house was open that he might keep his eye upon his clerk, who, in a dismal little cell beyond, a sort of tank, was copying letters. Scrooge had a very small fire, but the clerk's fire was so very much smaller that it looked like one coal. But he couldn't replenish it, for Scrooge kept the coal-box in his own room; and so surely as the clerk came in with the shovel, the master predicted that it would be necessary for them to part. Wherefore the clerk put on his white comforter, and tried to warm himself at the candle; in which effort, not being a man of strong imagination, he failed.

'A merry Christmas, uncle! God save you!' cried a cheerful voice. It was the voice of Scrooge's nephew, who came upon him so quickly that this was the first intimation he had of his approach.

'Bah!' said Scrooge, 'Humbug!'

What do you notice about the setting? the language and style?
How can you tell that the story was written a long time ago?

Note down your ideas.

Write on a separate sheet of paper.

Shakespeare

In literacy work this week the children have been finding out about the life and work of William Shakespeare and studying extracts from some of his plays. At word level they have investigated how the meaning of some words and expressions has changed over time.

Find out more about the life and work of William Shakespeare.

Here are some topics you could research.
• the theatre and acting in Shakespeare's time.
• Shakespeare's sonnets
• the building of the new Globe Theatre in London
• famous characters in Shakespeare's plays

Here are some ways of finding information.
• Go to your local public library.
• Look for books and CD Roms about Shakespeare and life in Elizabethan and Jacobean England.
• Look up Shakespeare in a Dictionary of Quotations.
• Use the Internet.

Here are some things you could do.
• Listen to audiocassette performances of Shakespeare's plays and readings of his poems. (You could borrow these from the library.)
• Watch films of Shakespeare's plays. (You could borrow these from the library or from a video hire shop.)

Viewpoint in fiction

In literacy work this week the children have been exploring the different points of view from which stories can be told and the different effects these create. They have been experimenting with different viewpoints in writing their own stories. At sentence level they have revised the use of pronouns. This week's work has also included preparation for English National Tests.

Answer these questions about a novel or short story that you have just finished reading.

Title _____   Author _____

1. Did you enjoy reading this story?

yes ☐   no ☐

Say what you liked or did not like about the story. Give your reasons.

_____

_____

_____

_____

2. Why do you think the author chose this title for the story?

_____

_____

Think of another title for the story.

_____

Explain why you think this would make a good title.

_____

_____

3. What is the most important moment in the story?

_____

_____

Give your reasons.

_____

_____

_____

Biography and autobiography

In literacy work this week the children have been investigating the differences between biograhical and autobiographical writing. They have written their own examples of these two kinds of non-fiction. At sentence level the focus has been on connecting words and phrases. At word level they have researched the origins of family names.

Choose pages in the telephone directory.

Scan them for names that belong in one of these four categories.

Write them down.

places	occupations
_____	_____
_____	_____
_____	_____
_____	_____
_____	_____
appearance/character	**parentage**
_____	_____
_____	_____
_____	_____
_____	_____
_____	_____

Write down other interesting surnames. Can you work out their origins?

Word derivations and origins

In literacy work this week the focus has been on word level work. The children have investigated families of related words and used dictionaries to find out the origins of words that have come into English from other languages.

Complete this chart by writing in words in the same family.

noun	adjective	verb
		manage
danger		
	beautiful	
origin		
		obey
		think
belief		
explosion		
	possessive	
		differ
	hard	
terror		
		criticise
	simple	
agreement		

Write down other noun/adjective/verb families.

Commentaries

In literacy work this week the children have written commentaries and summaries on fiction and non-fiction texts. They have also been preparing for National Tests in reading.

The sentence level focus has been on contracting sentences.

The word level focus has been on words with related spelling patterns.

Choose a word. _____

Write down 5 words that are related to it in different ways. Explain the link.

related word	kind of relationship
1	
2	
3	
4	
5	

Write a one-sentence summary of a chapter of a novel you have just read. _____

_____

_____

Write a short commentary on this chapter or on the novel so far.

_____

_____

_____

_____

Fiction genres

Literacy work this week has been concerned with the different kinds of fiction. Children have studied extracts from thrillers, science fiction, fantasy and historical novels.

The word level focus has been on spelling rules and the structure of complicated words.

Use this chart to write about the kind of fiction you like best. Explain the features of this kind of fiction, and why you like it. Quote some typical sentences.

GENRE _____

Some favourite books _____

_____

characters _____

_____

_____

Quotation _____

_____

_____

setting _____

_____

_____

Quotation _____

_____

_____

language _____

_____

_____

Quotation _____

_____

_____

Humorous verse

Literacy work this week has been concerned with humorous poems. Children have been reading a range of poems and investigating 'nonsense words'.
The word level focus has been on words with similar spelling patterns and structures.

Write your own dictionary definitions for the invented words in the first verse of Lewis Carroll's poem *Jabberwocky*. Add illustrations for the nouns on a separate sheet of paper.

'Twas brillig, and the slithy toves
Did gyre and gimble in the wabe:
All mimsy were the borogoves,
And the mome raths outgrabe.

brillig (adj)

slithy (adj)

gimble (vb)

wabe (n)

mimsy (adj)

borogove (n)

raths (n)

outgrabe (vb)

Narrative structure

Literacy work this week has been concerned with the structure of stories. Children have read stories in which time is organised in different ways, e.g. with flashbacks and dream sequences. The sentence level focus has been on shortening sentences without losing the sense.

Here are some long sentences about environmental issues. Make them shorter. Make them shorter again! Don't lose the main idea.

1. Some people would rather have 'organic' honey (the plants haven't been sprayed with chemicals) but the beekeepers stress that although the bees are encouraged to fly towards organically grown plants, there is no guarantee that they will end up there!

FIRST TRY _____

_____

SECOND TRY _____

2. If you don't live within walking distance, and if there is no school bus or reliable public transport, then you probably travel by car, which is one of the most environmentally damaging ways to get about.

FIRST TRY _____

_____

SECOND TRY _____

3. The labels of your clothes should tell you from which materials they have been made but it is difficult to say whether one is definitely a better choice for green consumers than another since there are *some* problems with all of them.

FIRST TRY _____

_____

SECOND TRY _____

Official language

In literacy work this week the children have studied the kind of language used in official notices and forms.
The sentence level focus has been on active and passive verbs and complex sentences.

Find and read a piece of official writing.
Try looking in catalogues and the paperwork that comes with things you buy.

Write down formal words and expressions.
How could you say it using less formal words?

The official text I read is _____

formal words and expressions	less formal way of saying it

Poetic devices

Literacy work this week has been concerned with poetic devices. Children have learned about how poets use similes and metaphors, the sounds of words and the ideas they evoke.
The sentence level focus has been on sentences with complex structures.
The word level focus has been on spelling patterns.

Choose pens, pencils or highlighters in two colours.
Use one colour to show how Ted Hughes uses the sounds of words in this poem.
Use the other colour to show how he uses similes and metaphors.

Wind

This house has been far out at sea all night,
The woods crashing through darkness, the booming hills,
Winds stampeding the fields under the window
Floundering black astride and blinding wet

Till day rose; then under an orange sky
The hills had new places, and wind wielded
Blade-light, luminous and emerald,
Flexing like the lens of a mad eye.

At noon I scaled along the house-side as far as
The coal-house door. I dared once to look up —
Through the brunt wind that dented the balls of my eyes
The tent of the hills drummed and strained its guy-rope,

The fields quivering, the skyline a grimace,
At any second to bang and vanish with a flap:
The wind flung a magpie away and a black-
Back gull bent like an iron bar slowly. The house

Rang like some fine green goblet in the note
That any second would shatter it. Now deep
In chairs, in front of the great fire, we grip
Our hearts and cannot entertain book, thought,

Or each other. We watch the fire blazing,
And feel the roots of the house move, but sit on,
Seeing the window tremble to come in,
Hearing the stones cry out under the horizons.

Ted Hughes

Poetic forms

Literacy work this week has been concerned with forms of poetry. Children have read poems with different rhyme schemes and different arrangements of syllables and used them as models for their own writing.

The sentence level focus has been on sentences with complex structures.

The word level focus has been on how the meaning of some words has changed over time.

Here are four haiku about winter – but the lines have got muddled up! Cut out the lines and try to arrange them to make the four original poems. Write them out

WARNING! These haiku do not obey the rules exactly.

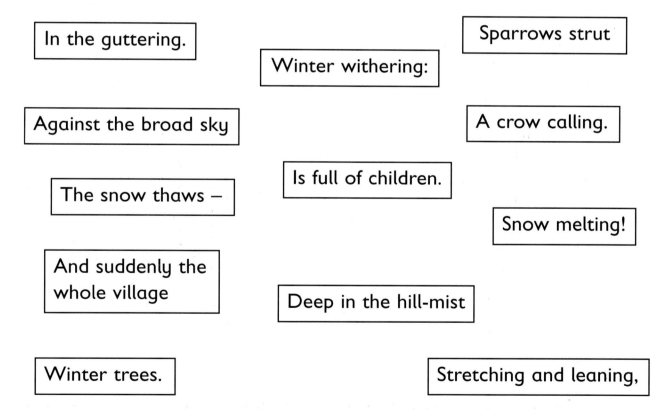

In the guttering.

Winter withering:

Sparrows strut

Against the broad sky

A crow calling.

The snow thaws –

Is full of children.

Snow melting!

And suddenly the whole village

Deep in the hill-mist

Winter trees.

Stretching and leaning,

Now experiment! See if you make any poems by rearranging these lines. Write them out.

Proverbs

In literacy work this week the children have been collecting and investigating proverbs.
The sentence level focus has been on contracting sentences.
The word level focus has been on how the meaning of some words has changed over time.

It is not always easy to work out the meaning of a proverb!
Write a short explanation of these.

Paddle your own canoe. _____
_____
_____

Better an egg today than a hen tomorrow.
_____
_____

The best fish swim near the bottom.
_____
_____

Take the bull by the horns.
_____
_____

The pot called the kettle black.
_____
_____

On a separate sheet of paper write down favourite proverbs that people in your family know.

Argument

> Literacy work this week has been concerned with argument and discussion.
> Children have read and evaluated texts that put forward one point of view and
> texts that give a balanced discussion.
> The sentence level focus has been on conditional sentences.
> The word level focus has been on connecting words for arguments and discussions.

Find and read a piece of writing that puts forward one particular point of view.

Answer these questions about it.

What is the issue? _____

_____

_____

What is the writer's point of view? _____

_____

_____

What arguments does the writer put forward for this point of view?
List them. _____

_____

_____

_____

How does the writer support these arguments (with examples? with
evidence?)? _____

_____

_____

_____

What do you think about the writer's point of view? ___

_____

_____

_____

Word play

In literacy work this week the children have been having fun with words! They have played word games, invented new words, tried to solve word puzzles and made up their own. This has involved investigating the structure of words and sentences.

Work out the meaning of these phone-text messages.

B4 _____

CU L8R _____

H8 _____

Msg _____

NE1 _____

OIC _____

PLS _____

PPL _____

RUOK _____

SOME1 _____

WAN2 _____

WOT RU Doin 2nite? _____

Try abbreviating other words and short messages like this.

Advertisements

In literacy work this week the children have been carrying out a detailed language investigation of advertisements. They have explored how words are chosen and sentences structured to create particular effects.
The word level focus has been on extending vocabulary and experimenting with language.

Look in newspapers and magazines to find an interesting advertisement.
Use this chart to record your ideas about it.

product
main selling points
use of language •   jingles and catch-phrases   •   word choice   •   word play   •   metaphors and similes   •   sentence structure   •   unconventional spellings

Comparing novelists

In literacy work this week the children have been studying and comparing the work of two novelists. They have also been learning to use a reading journal to note their ideas and responses.

The sentence level focus has been on the features of narrative writing and on complex sentences.

Use this chart to compare the work of two other novelists you enjoy reading.

NOVELIST 1 _____	NOVELIST 2 _____
themes and ideas	
action	
characters	
setting	
language	
tone	

Explanatory texts

In literacy work this week the children have been studying the features of explanatory texts and writing their own explanations.
The sentence level focus has been on formal styles of writing.
The word level focus has been on identifying and correcting spelling mistakes.

This diagram shows the Greenhouse Effect.

Write an explanation of the process – without using pictures.

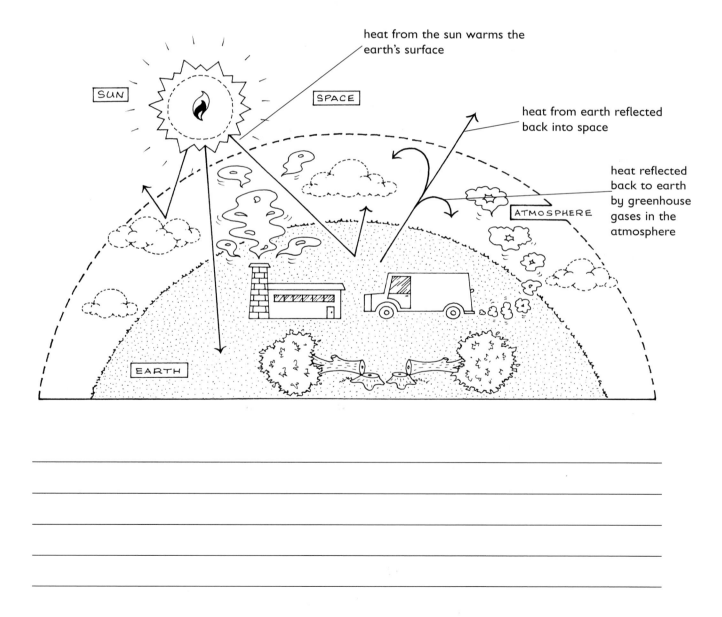

heat from the sun warms the earth's surface

heat from earth reflected back into space

heat reflected back to earth by greenhouse gases in the atmosphere

SUN

SPACE

ATMOSPHERE

EARTH

_____

_____

_____

_____

_____

Extended story

In literacy work this week the children have been planning, writing and revising a long story. They developed plot, ideas, characters and setting.
The sentence level focus has been on the structure and punctuation of complex sentences. The word level focus has been on identifying and correcting mis-spelt words, on extending vocabulary and experimenting with similes and metaphors.

Someone has copied out this extract from Jules Verne's science-fiction story *Voyage to the Centre of the Earth* – and made lots of spelling mistakes.
Circle the mis-spelt words. Write the correct spelling above. On another sheet of paper, explain what the problem is and why the writer might have made this mistake.

Tuesday, August 20. At last it is evening – the time of day when we feel a grate need to sleep.

Of coarse, in this continueing light there is no nite, but we are very tired. Hans remains at the

rudder, his eyes never closed. I don't know when he sleeps; but I find I am dozeing myslef.

And then . . . an awfull shock! the raft seems to have struck some hiden rock. It is liftted

right out of the water and even seems to be thrown some distence. "Eh!" crys my uncle.

"What's happening?" And Hans raises his hand and points to where, abowt two hundred yards

away, a great black mass is heaveing. Then I know my worst feers have been realised.

"It's some . . . monster!" I cry . . .

"And a wale!" the Professor shouts. "See those enormus fins! And see how it blows the

water!"

And indeed two colums of water rise from the serface of the sea as he speaks, reaching an

immence hight before they fall back into the sea with an enormus crash. The whole cave in

which this great sea is set, its walls and roof invisable to us, echos with the sound of it.

Linked poems

In literacy work this week the children have been reading, comparing and writing sequences of linked poems.
The sentence level focus has been on the structure of complex sentences.
The word level focus has been on experimenting with similes and metaphors.

This is how three poems from T. S. Eliot's *Old Possum's Book of Practical Cats* begin.

Macavity: The Mystery cat

Macavity's a Mystery Cat: he's called the Hidden Paw –
For he's the master criminal who can defy the law.
He's the bafflement of Scotland Yard, the Flying Squad's despair:
For when they reach the scene of crime – *Macavity's not there!*

Skimbleshanks: The Railway cat

There's a whisper down the line at 11.39
When the Night Mail's ready to depart,
Saying, 'Skimble where is Skimble has he gone to hunt the thimble?
We must find him or the train can't start.'

Bustopher Jones: The Cat about Town

Bustopher Jones is *not* skin and bones –
In fact, he's remarkably fat.
He doesn't haunt pubs – he has eight or nine clubs,
For he's the St James's Street Cat!

On a separate sheet of paper write a description of the ways in which these three poems are linked.

Think especially about:
- subject
- rhyme
- rhythm
- tone and humour

Range of non-fiction texts

In literacy work this week the children have been reading and writing different kinds of non-fiction texts, including explanations, instructions, reports and persuasive writing.
The sentence level focus has been on the grammatical features of these texts, and on formal styles of writing.

How could you write about this windmill?

- an explanation?   • persuasive writing?   • a non-chronological report?
- instructions?   • a recount?

Write short texts about the windmill in as many different styles as you can.
You will need to use your imagination and make up some information!

Reference texts

In literacy work this week the children have been investigating and using different kinds of reference books, including dictionaries, thesauruses and encyclopaedias. They have studied the information they provide and how this is organised.
The sentence level focus has been on formal styles of writing, which they have used to write their own reference texts.
The word level focus has been on extending vocabulary.

Look at this fantasy creature.

DROGGLE

FUMMLE

On a separate sheet of paper write an encyclopaedia entry about it.
You will need to: • give it a name
• describe how it lives – how it moves, what it eats …
• describe where it lives

Then write dictionary definitions for the two parts of its body which are labelled.

Reviews

In literacy work this week the children have been reading and writing book reviews.
They have also written summaries and synopses of books.
The sentence level focus has been on formal styles of writing.
The word level focus has been on choosing precise and accurate words.

Write a review of something that you really like. It could be:

• a TV programme   • a film   • a magazine or comic   • a pop song

Think about:

Who you are writing for:
- what do they need to know?
- what would they be interested in?

What you want to say:
- what is it about?
- what did you like about it? Why?
- what makes it special?
- how did it make you feel?
- what did it make you think about?

How you are going to write and organise your review:
- in paragraphs?
- as a poster?
- using quotations?

Use a separate sheet of paper to write your review.

Study of an individual poet

In literacy work this week the children have been studying the work of the poet _____.
They have read and compared poems, and written reviews.
The sentence level focus has been on formal styles of writing.
The word level focus has been on choosing precise and vivid words.

Here are four short poems by the American poet Ogden Nash.

The Octopus

Tell me, O Octopus, I begs,
Is those things arms, or is they legs?
I marvel at thee, Octopus:
If I were thou, I'd call me Us.

The Pig

The pig, if I am not mistaken,
Supplies us sausage, ham and bacon.
Let others say his heart is big —
I call it stupid of the pig.

Reflection on Ingenuity

Here's a good rule of thumb:
Too clever is dumb.

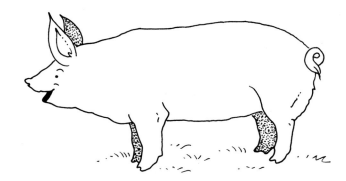

The Cow

The cow is of the bovine ilk;
One end is moo, the other, milk.

What can you tell about Ogden Nash's work from these poems?
Think about:
- how he uses words
- what amuses him
- what he is interested in
- the structure of his poems.

Write a short description of his work on a separate sheet of paper.

Notes

Notes